D1559338

Christianity
and
The New Age

WORKS BY CHRISTOPHER DAWSON

The Age of the Gods
Beyond Politics
The Crisis of Western Education
Christianity and the New Age
Christianity in East & West
The Dividing of Christendom
The Dynamics of World History
Enquiries into Religion and Culture
The Formation of Christendom
The Gods of Revolution
The Historic Reality of Christian Culture
Judgment of the Nations
The Making of Europe
Medieval Essays
Medieval Religion and Other Essays
Mission to Asia
The Modern Dilemma
The Movement of World Revolution
Progress and Religion
Religion and Culture
Religion and the Modern State
Religion and the Rise of Western Culture
Religion and World History
The Revolt of Asia
The Spirit of the Oxford Movement
Understanding Europe

Christianity
and
The New Age

by

Christopher Dawson

Introduction by John J. Mulloy

Sophia Institute Press
Manchester, New Hampshire

Christianity and the New Age was originally published by Sheed and Ward in 1931.

Introduction, Biography, and Index
Copyright © 1985 Sophia Institute

Printed in the United States of America
All rights reserved.

Second Printing 1988

Cover design by Susan Barger

Nihil obstat
Arthur J. Scanlan, S.T.D.
Censor Librorum

Imprimatur
+ Patrick Cardinal Hayes
Archbishop, New York
April 21, 1931

Library of Congress Cataloging in Publication Data

Dawson, Christopher, 1889-1970
  Christianity and the new age.

  Reprint. Originally published: London:
      Sheed & Ward, 1931.
  Includes bibliographical references and index.
  1. Christianity and culture. 2. Christianity—20th century.
      3. Civilization, Modern—20th century.
      4. Humanism—Controversial literature.
      5. Civilization, Secular. I. Title.
BR115.C8D29 1985   261   84-29821
    ISBN 0-918477-01-8 (pbk.)
    ISBN 0-918477-02-6 (hdbk.)

CONTENTS

Introduction

by John J. Mulloy

There are moments when the obscurity of history seems to be suddenly illuminated by some sign of divine purpose. These are the moments of crisis in the literal sense of the word—times of judgement when the powers of this world are tried and condemned and when the course of history suddenly flows into a new channel. Such was the age of the Hebrew prophets, such was the age of St. Augustine, and such is the age in which we have the privilege and the misfortune to live today. For the present century has been an apocalyptic age—a time of judgement in which the established powers and authorities of the world have been put through the fire and destroyed or renewed, and when civilizations that have endured for thousands of years are being forced into a new mold.[1]

Drawing upon history and philosophy as well as upon the social sciences (including anthropology, sociology, social psychology, politics, and economics), Christopher Dawson's *Christianity and the New Age* brilliantly analyzes our apocalyptic contemporary age. It sets the social problems of our age in the

[1] Christopher Dawson, *The Movement of World Revolution* (N.Y.: Sheed and Ward, 1959), p. 102.

context of mankind's cultural history, establishing certain permanent principles of human nature and human society which are essential for any reconstruction of the social order today.

Our modern age *is* apocalyptic. Nonetheless, in this work Christopher Dawson shows that it is not cut off from its past but is organically related to what has gone before.

Dawson does this by focusing on humanism, which is this work's unifying theme. He shows that humanist values owe much of their power and ascendancy over the modern mind to the earlier formative influence of Christianity upon Western social attitudes. At the same time, he reveals how humanist values have been transformed by contemporary thought and the conditions of modern society.

Dawson devotes the first and last chapters of *Christianity and the New Age* to a consideration of the particular challenges to Christianity found in contemporary thought, especially in the writings of Marx, Nietzsche, D. H. Lawrence, J. Middleton Murry, and Irving Babbitt. He sharpens this picture by contrasting Christianity and humanism with the Oriental world religions and with modern ideologies.

This contrast is especially brought out in the middle

two chapters of *Christianity and the New Age*, where Dawson brilliantly synthesizes the religious history of mankind. These are possibly the most concise and penetrating chapters he has ever written, going beyond even the masterful achievement of his *Progress and Religion*.

In these chapters, Dawson brings together in a unified picture the religious aspirations of primitive man, the insights of the Oriental world religions, the essentials of Christianity, the Catholic principles of belief on which the early Christian community was founded, the development of Protestantism (from Luther to Harnack and Schweitzer), and some of the modern "substitutes" for Christianity.

In his conclusion, Dawson shows how Catholic Christianity occupies a middle ground between the characteristic values and typical excesses of both East and West, combining the particular truths of each in a higher and more comprehensive synthesis.

In brief, the following elements constitute the special contributions of *Christianity and the New Age*:

1) The Roots of Humanism in Christianity

This book shows the key importance of humanism for the development of Western culture, but a humanism transformed by Christianity. It analyzes the basic difference between Christian humanism and a humanism which is man-centered and consequently self-defeating. Thus, Dawson notes in Chapter I,

> . . . we have the paradox that at the beginning of the Renaissance, when the conquest of nature and the creation of modern science are still unrealized, man appears in godlike freedom with a sense of unbounded power and greatness; while at the end of the nineteenth century, when nature has been conquered and there seem no limits to the powers of science, man is once more conscious of his misery and weakness as the slave of material circumstance and physical appetite and death. Instead of the heroic exaltation of humanity which was characteristic of the naturalism of the Renaissance, we see the humiliation of humanity. . . . Man is stripped of his glory and freedom and left as a naked human animal shivering in an inhuman universe. (pp. 9–10)

Dawson sees this to be the necessary consequence of any *strictly secular* humanism. For, as he shows in this book, even secular humanism in Western culture derives much of its inspiration from the Christian ethos. Thus, any attempt to eliminate Christianity or restrict its social influence cuts the roots of humanism's own source of life.

2) The Essential Affinity Between Christianity and Science

Christianity and the New Age describes the essential affinity which exists between Christian humanism and scientific investigation. Dawson argues that ". . . the material organization of the world by science and invention is in no sense to be refused or despised by the Catholic tradition, for to the Catholic philosopher no less than to the scientist the progressive *rationalization* of matter by the work of scientific intelligence is the natural vocation of the human mind." (pp. 94–95) In other words, it is not at all a matter of chance that science has come to its full fruition in a culture whose basic values have been formed by Christianity.

3) The Unity of Mankind's Religious Aspirations and Experiences

Christianity and the New Age surveys the whole of mankind's religious experience, and from this perspective identifies two fundamental needs of the human soul at all stages of culture: ". . . God, the supernatural, the transcendent . . . (and) . . . deliverance, salvation, eternal life." (p. 22) And, says Dawson, "both these two elements are represented in some form or other in any given religion." (p. 22)

With regard to the first element, Dawson points out that "primitive man had already found the Transcendent immanent in and working through nature as the supernatural." (p. 38) On the other hand, the Oriental world religions "isolated (the transcendent) and set it over against the world of human experience . . . as Reality against Appearance, and as the Spiritual against the Sensible." (p. 38)

In contrast to both of these, Christianity united a strong sense of the transcendent character of Ultimate Reality with the belief that God had become man. "This conception of the Incarnation as the bridge between God and Man, the marriage of Heaven and Earth, the channel through which the material world is spiritualized and brought back to unity, distinguishes Christianity from all the other Oriental religions, and involves a completely new attitude to life." (pp. 82–83)

4) The Tradition of Israel and The Mission and Teaching of Jesus

Christianity and the New Age shows how the mission and teaching of Jesus gave a deeper and more spiritual meaning to the tradition of Israel concerning the promised Messiah and His work of redemption. Also, it shows that (contrary to later Protestant claims) Jesus in the Gospel preached a *dogmatic* and *sacramental* religion, whose characteristics immediately became embodied in the religious practices of the early Christian community.

5) Protestantism and the Self-Contradictions of Radical Biblical Criticism

Christianity and the New Age identifies some of the main features in the development of Protestantism from the sixteenth to the twentieth century, especially regarding its attitude toward the Bible. In connection with Harnack and Liberal Protestantism, it presents an incisive critique of radical Biblical criticism, and notes that such criticism is guilty of precisely those faults which it claimed to be eliminating from the traditional Christian understanding of the Bible.

6) The Messianic Character and Radical Insufficiency of Marxism

Christianity and the New Age also contains an analysis of the nature of Communism which shows that it is not rooted in the natural order of the universe but in the psychology of Karl Marx. Dawson indicates the motives which lead men to accept Marxism and the needs which Marxism attempts to satisfy. But he also illustrates the radical insufficiency of Marxism as an explanation either of history, economics, or society, showing that its widespread appeal is based not on Marxism's own worldview, but upon Messianic elements which it has borrowed from the Jewish Prophetic tradition. These elements are in striking contradiction to the basic premises of the Marxist materialist interpretation of history.

7) The Theological Roots of the Unique Dynamic Character of Christian Culture

Finally, *Christianity and the New Age* illustrates the dynamic character of Western culture, which makes it unique among the civilizations of the world. For Christianity infused a wholly new spirit and a new conception of reality into the civilization of the West. As Dawson points out in his concluding chapter, Christendom "cannot escape from the contagion of the divine fire that has been kindled in its midst. Why is it that Europe alone among the civilizations of the world has been continually shaken and transformed by an energy of spiritual unrest that refuses to be content with the unchanging law of social tradition which rules the Oriental cultures? It is because its religious ideal has not been the worship of timeless and changeless perfection, but a spirit that strives to incorporate itself in humanity and to change the world." (pp. 86–87)

Therefore, says Christopher Dawson in his moving conclusion of this brilliant little book,

> Every Christian mind is a seed of change so long as it is a living mind, not enervated by custom or ossified by prejudice. A Christian has only to *be* in order to change the world, for in that act of being there is contained all the mystery of supernatural life. It is the function of the Church to sow this divine seed to produce not merely good men, but spiritual men—that is to say, supermen. In so far as the Church fulfills this function it transmits to the world a continuous stream of spiritual energy. If the salt itself loses its savor, then indeed the world sinks back into disorder and death, for a despiritualized Christianity is powerless to change anything; it is the most abject of failures, since it serves neither the natural nor the spiritual order. But the life of the Church never fails, since it possesses an infinite capacity for regeneration. It is the external organ through which the Spirit enters the social process and builds up a new humanity—*populus qui nascetur quem fecit Dominus*. The spirit breathes and they are created and the face of the earth is renewed.

Christianity
and
The New Age

Chapter I
Humanism and the New Order[1]

For centuries a civilization will follow the same path, worshipping the same gods, cherishing the same ideals, acknowledging the same moral and intellectual standards. And then all at once a change will come, the springs of the old life run dry, and men suddenly awake to a new world, in which the ruling principles of the former age seem to lose their validity and to become inapplicable or meaningless.

This is what occurred in the time of the Roman Empire, when the ancient world, which had lived for centuries on the inherited capital of the Hellenistic culture, seemed suddenly to come to the end of its resources and to realize its need of something entirely

[1] The author desires to express his thanks to the editors and publishers of the *Criterion* and the *Dublin Review* for their kindness in allowing him to reprint, in the first two chapters of this essay, portions of articles which originally appeared in the pages of those reviews.

new. For four hundred years the civilized world had been reading the same books, admiring the same works of art, and cultivating the same types of social and personal expression. Then came the change of the third and fourth centuries, A.D., when the forms of the Hellenistic culture suddenly lost their vitality and men turned to a new art, a new thought and a new way of life — from philosophy to theology, from the Greek statue to the Byzantine mosaic, from the gymnasium to the monastery.

This species of cultural discontinuity is not unknown in other civilizations — for example in China in the third and fourth centuries A.D. — but it seems specially characteristic of the West. It took place once more in the fifteenth and sixteenth centuries at the close of the Middle Ages, and we seem to be experiencing something of the kind in Europe today. During the last period of the nineteenth century and the first years of the twentieth century a further phase of Western civilization came to an end. The old capital was exhausted and there was nothing to take its place. Liberalism and Nationalism had won their long fight with the old order, but they had lost their own ideals. In Italy the Risorgimento had given place to the age of Crispi and the Triple Alliance, and in France the centenary of the Republic was being celebrated by the Panama scandals. It was a dark age—dark not as in the early Middle Ages with the honest night of barbarism, but with the close uneasy gloom that comes before a storm. In the past, the periods of climax, as a rule, have been ages of material distress and economic decline, but the terrifying thing about that age was its prosperity, its confidence, its material success. "There has never," wrote Péguy,

> been an age in which money was to such a degree the only master and god. And never have the rich been so protected against the poor and the poor so unprotected against the rich. . . .
>
> And never has the temporal been so protected against the spiritual; and never has the spiritual been so unprotected against the temporal.[2]

The goal of the Liberal Enlightenment and Revolution had been reached, and Europe at last possessed a completely secularized culture. The old religion had not been destroyed; in fact throughout Protestant Europe the churches still possessed a position of established privilege. But they held this position only on the condition that they did not interfere with the reign of Mammon. In reality they had been pushed aside into a

---

[2] C. Péguy, *L'argent Suite*, pp. 170–171.

backwater where they were free to stagnate in peace and to brood over the memory of dead controversies which had moved the mind of Europe three centuries before.

On the other hand the intellectuals who had contributed so much to the victory of the new order of things were in a somewhat similar plight. They found themselves powerless to influence the movement of civilization, which had cut itself free, not only from tradition, but also from art and thought. The spiritual leadership that was possessed by Voltaire and Rousseau, by Goethe and Fichte, was now a thing of the past. The men of letters were expected to follow society, not to lead it. And this is what many of them did, whether with the professional servility of the journalist or with the disinterested fanaticism of the realist, who affirmed his artistic integrity by the creation of an imaginary world no less devoid of spiritual significance than was the social world in which he lived. But a large number, probably the majority, found neither of these alternatives satisfactory. They turned to literature and art as a means of escape from reality. That was the meaning to many of the catchword, "Art for Art's sake."[3] Symbolism and aestheticism, the Ivory

---

[3] Its true meaning, however, is to be found rather in the dillettantism of Oscar Wilde.

4

Tower and the Celtic Twilight, Satanism and the cult of "Evil," hashish and absinthe; all of them were ways by which the last survivors of Romanticism made their escape, leaving the enemy in possession of the field.

There was, however, one exception, one man who refused to surrender.

Whatever his weakness Friedrich Nietzsche was neither a time-server nor a coward. He at least stood for the supremacy of spirit, when so many of those whose office it was to defend it had fallen asleep or had gone over to the enemy. He remained faithful to the old ideals of the Renaissance culture, the ideals of creative genius and of the self-affirmation of the free personality, and he revolted against the blasphemies of an age which degraded the personality and denied the power of the spirit in the name of humanity and liberty.

Nevertheless, Nietzsche himself was far from being a humanist. Humanism is essentially a *via media*, and in the nineteenth century the *via media* had become identical with mediocrity. In Nietzsche's eyes humanity had become something either ridiculous or shameful, and the attempt to pass beyond humanity led him to the negation of humanism and the destruction of his own personality; as he said, the way of the creator is to burn himself in his own fire. Yet the tragedy of Nietzsche is the tragedy of the end of humanism, since it only reveals with exceptional clearness the ultimate consequences of the antinomy that was inherent in the humanist tradition from the beginning.

The essentially transitory character of the humanist culture has been obscured by the dominance of the belief in Progress and by the shallow and dogmatic optimism which characterized nineteenth-century Liberalism. It was only an exceptionally original mind, like that of the late T. E. Hulme, that could free itself from the influence of Liberal dogma and could recognize *the signs of the times* — the passing of the ideals that had dominated European civilization for four centuries, and the dawn of a new order.

In the years that followed the war this consciousness has become general, at least on the Continent, owing largely to the popularity of Spengler's well-known book, *The Decline of the West*. But Spengler's arbitrary and subjective theorizing threw no light upon the inner meaning of the change. A much more profound analysis of the modern situation is to be found in the works of the modern Russian thinkers of the school of Solovyov, above all Nicholas Berdyaev. In his book *Der Sinn der Geschichte* and in his later essays on

"The New Middle Ages," Berdyaev has dealt with the passing of humanism not as an instance of historical fatality, but in its ultimate significance for the spiritual life of humanity, and has shown how the disintegration of the Renaissance culture was the result of a spiritual disunity and conflict which it was never able to overcome.

In spite of its ideal of a purely human perfection and its cult of classical form, there was in humanism something excessive, a kind of *hubris* which led it to destruction. We see this already in the brilliant culture of fifteenth-century Italy, where the unbridled individualism of princes and cities led to the loss of national independence. But that is only a superficial instance of the instability of the new order. It is not in any obvious material failure, but in its very triumphs and successes, that the real weakness of the movement is to be found. For each fresh victory of the humanistic spirit undermined the foundations of its own vitality.

The Renaissance has its beginning in the self-discovery, the self-realization and the self-exaltation of Man. Medieval man had attempted to base his life on the supernatural. His ideal of knowledge was not the adventurous quest of the human mind exploring its own kingdom; it was an intuition of the eternal verities which is itself an emanation from the Divine Intellect — *irradiatio et participatio primae lucis*. The men of the Renaissance, on the other hand, turned away from the eternal and the absolute to the world of nature and human experience. They rejected their dependence on the supernatural, and vindicated their independence and supremacy in the temporal order. But thereby they were gradually led by an internal process of logic to criticize the principles of their own knowledge and to lose confidence in their own freedom. The self-affirmation of man gradually led to the denial of the spiritual foundations of his freedom and knowledge. This tendency shows itself in every department of modern thought. In philosophy, it leads from the dogmatic rationalism of Descartes and the dogmatic empiricism of Locke to the radical skepticism of Hume and the subjectivism of later German thought. Reason is gradually stripped of its prerogatives until nothing is left to it but the bare "as if" of Vaihinger.

In science, the growth of man's knowledge and his control over nature is accompanied by a growing sense of man's dependence on material forces. He gradually loses his position of exception and superiority and sinks back into nature. He becomes a subordinate part of the great mechanical system that his scientific genius has created. In the same way, the economic process, which led to the exploitation of the world by man and the vast increase of his material resources, ends in the subjection of man to the rule of the machine and the mechanization of human life. Finally, in the political and social sphere, the revolt against the medieval principle of hierarchy and the reassertion of the rights of the secular power led to the absolutism of the modern national state. This again was followed by a second revolt—the assertion of the rights of man against secular authority which culminated in the French Revolution. But this second revolt also led to disillusion. It led, on the one hand, to the disintegration of the organic principle in society into an individualistic atomism, which leaves the individual isolated and helpless before the new economic forces, and, on the other, to the growth of the new bureaucratic state, that "coldest of cold monsters," which exerts a more irresistible and far-reaching control over the individual life than was ever possessed by the absolute monarchies of the old regime.

So we have the paradox that at the beginning of the Renaissance, when the conquest of nature and the creation of modern science are still unrealized, man appears in god-like freedom with a sense of unbounded

power and greatness; while at the end of the nineteenth century, when nature has been conquered and
there seem no limits to the powers of science, man is
once more conscious of his misery and weakness as the
slave of material circumstance and physical appetite
and death. Instead of the heroic exaltation of humanity
which was characteristic of the naturalism of the
Renaissance, we see the humiliation of humanity in
the anti-human naturalism of Zola. Man is stripped of
his glory and freedom and left as a naked human
animal shivering in an inhuman universe.

Thus humanism by its own inner development is
eventually brought to deny itself and to pass away into
its opposite. For Nietzsche, who refused to surrender
the spiritual element in the Renaissance tradition,
humanism is transcended in an effort to attain to the
superhuman without abandoning the self-assertion
and the rebellious freedom of the individual will—an
attempt which inevitably ends in self-destruction. But
modern civilization as a whole could not follow this
path. It naturally chose to live as best it could, rather
than to commit a spectacular suicide. And so, in order
to adapt itself to the new conditions, it was forced to
throw over the humanist tradition.

Hence the increasing acceptance of the mechanization

of life that has characterized the last thirty years.
Above all, in the period since the war there has been a
growing tendency towards the de-intellectualization
and exteriorization of European life. The old fixed
canons of social and moral conduct have been aban-
doned, and society has given itself up to the current of
external change without any attempt towards self-
direction or the preservation of spiritual continuity.
But this acceptance of new conditions is in itself
negative, and possesses no creative quality. It points to
the dying-down and stagnation of culture rather than
its renewal. Nor is this surprising. For centuries,
Western civilization has received its impetus from the
humanist tradition, and the dying-away of that tradition naturally involves the temporary cessation of
cultural creativeness.

From this point of view it is very significant that
almost the only original element in the thought of the
new age should be the work of Jews. In physical science the dominant figure is Einstein, in psychology it
is Freud, in economics and sociology it is Marx — and
each of them has exerted an influence on the thought
of the age that far transcends the limits of his particular
subject. And it is easy to understand the reasons for
this. The Jewish mind alone in the West has its own

sources of life which are independent of the Hellenic and the Renaissance traditions. It has seen too many civilizations rise and fall to be discouraged by the failure of humanism. On the contrary it thrives in an atmosphere of determinism and historical destiny, which seems fatal to the humanist spirit. This holds good especially of the Marxian attitude, which is characteristic of the new conditions, although it originated at a time when liberalism and romanticism were still flourishing. But Marx addressed himself to those elements in the modern world which were already deprived of any share in the heritage of humanist culture. He found the proletariat enslaved to the machine, and he sought, not to destroy this servitude, but to equalize and rationalize it by extending it to the whole social organism.

Thus, in Marx, the cult of equality and social justice led to the sacrifice of human freedom and spiritual creativeness to an inhuman economic whole. He condemned the whole humanistic morality and culture as bourgeois, and accepted the machine, not only as the basis of economic activity, but as the explanation of the mystery of life itself. The mechanical processes of economic life are the ultimate realities of history and human life. All other things—religion, art, philosophy, spiritual life—stand on a lower plane of reality; they are a dream world of shadows cast on the sleeping mind by the physical processes of the real world of matter and mechanism. Hence Marxism may be seen as the culminating point of the modern tendency to explain that which is specifically human in terms of something else. For the Marxian interpretation of history is in fact nothing but an explaining away of history. It professes to guide us to the heart of the problem, and it merely unveils a void. And thus, according to Berdyaev, the essential importance of Marxism is to be found not in its constructive proposals, but in its negations, its sweeping away of the semi-ideological constructions of nineteenth-century thought. For the optimistic rationalism of the nineteenth century tended to hide the true significance of the conflict between materialism and spiritualism. Just as behind all religion and all spiritual philosophy there is a metaphysical assent—the affirmation of Being—so behind materialism and the materialist explaining away of history there is a metaphysical negation—the denial of Being—which is the ultimate and quasi-mystical ground of the materialistic position. In Berdyaev's words, "Man must either incorporate himself in this mystery of Not-being, and sink in the abyss of Not-being,

or he must return to the inner mystery of human
destiny and unite himself once again with the sacred
traditions" that are the true basis of the historical process.[4]

The Western observer will probably question the
metaphysical importance which Berdyaev attributes to
the Marxian doctrine. It is, however, impossible to
deny the connection between Communism and historical materialism, and the former actually derives much
of its moral driving force from a quasi-religious devotion to the materialistic theory. There is no mistaking
the note of somber religious enthusiasm that charac-
terizes, for example, Lenin's attitude to the metaphysical side of the Marxian creed. When he attacks Mach
for having "betrayed materialism with a kiss," he is
not speaking in jest. He is condemning what he regards as an act of spiritual apostasy.

But this attitude finds a much more congenial atmosphere in Russia, where the religious impulse has
always had a tendency towards Nihilism, than in the
West. In Western Europe the decadence of the humanist tradition has left the European mind so weak that it
is no longer capable of any metaphysical conviction.
The greatest danger here is not that we should actively

[4] Berdyaev, *Der Sinn der Geschichte*, pp. 34–35.

adopt the Bolshevik cult of Marxian materialism, but rather that we should yield ourselves passively to a practical materialization of culture after the American pattern. The Communists may have deified mechanism in theory, but it is the Americans who have realized it in practice. They have adapted themselves to the conditions of the new age earlier and more completely than the peoples of the Old World, partly because the external circumstances of American life were more favorable, but most of all because they were spiritually more independent of the humanist tradition. The Renaissance culture that had its center in the courts and capitals of Europe left America almost untouched. The American tradition is founded on Calvinism, which governed the social life of the Northern States down to the nineteenth century, and which possessed an almost complete monopoly of higher education; while in the new lands outside the old colonial territory, the churches, whether Calvinist or Baptist or Methodist, were still all-important, and humanist education, which was still so powerful in Europe, was practically non-existent.

Now the social effect of Calvinism and of American Protestantism in general is to create an immensely strong moral motive for action without any corresponding intellectual ideal. It is a culture of the will rather than of the understanding — a purely ethical discipline which neglects intellectual and aesthetic values. This attitude remains characteristic of American civilization even in its secular development. Thus the ideals of humanist democracy, which were received from France in the revolutionary period, were stripped of their intellectual element and moralized as a justification for the unregulated activity of the ordinary man. This led, on the one hand, to the individualistic cult of material success and, on the other, to a humanitarian idealism that is in reality nothing else but the same ideal in a socialized form. No doubt these ideals still preserved some of the moral inspiration that derives from the Puritan tradition, just as European liberalism retained something of the humanist tradition. But when this religious inspiration has evaporated, American civilization without Calvinism, like modern European civilization without humanism, becomes a body without a soul. And it is this dead civilization which is apotheosized in the mythology of Hollywood and which is invading the Old World with all the prestige of its vast material achievement. It possesses a kind of pseudo-humanist appeal since it offers the ordinary man and woman the vision of a wider and richer life. The new machine-made civilization may be destructive of the finer pleasures in life, but under the old conditions these were only accessible to a small number. The ordinary man gets more satisfaction from his cinema and his daily paper than from grand opera or classical literature. If modern civilization is able to pay its way, if it is not upset by some unexpected economic or military catastrophe, we have no reason to suppose that it will be undermined by any movement of popular dissatisfaction. On the contrary, the whole tendency of democratic politics and social reform and economic progress is to extend the sway of this standardized industrial mass-civilization. Nor can education improve matters, since if the teacher himself is without a humanist tradition or a spiritual discipline he cannot impart them to others. And science is equally unhelpful, since, when it is once separated from the humanist tradition, it becomes as utilitarian and materialistic as industrialism. The ordinary man knows and cares nothing for it, and the leader of industry and the politician value it only as the servant of the machine. The only remedy is to be found in man himself—in the renewal of the human image which was once impressed so clearly on our Western civilization, but which has now become disfigured and effaced.

Chapter II
Humanism and Religious Experience

The realization of the decline of the humanist tradition and the prospect of the complete mechanization of our civilization have produced a striking change in the modern intellectual attitude towards religion. The last generation—the generation of H. G. Wells and Bernard Shaw—was still prepared to idealize the machine and to place its hopes in a mechanized Utopia. The present generation has lost this confidence and is beginning to feel the need for a return to religion and a recovery of the religious attitude to life which the European mind has lost during the last two or three centuries.

And this feeling is no longer confined to the Conservatives and the supporters of the traditional intellectual order, as was largely the case in the last century. On the contrary, it is especially characteristic of the most modern of the moderns and of those who are in revolt against the existing order of things—of men like the late D. H. Lawrence and Mr. Middleton Murry and Mr. T. S. Eliot in this country, of Hugo Ball and Stefan Georg in Germany, and of Jacques Rivière, Charles du Bos and François Mauriac in France.

In the latter country alone it has taken the form of a complete acceptance of orthodox Catholicism. Elsewhere, and especially in England, it still retains to a great extent the ideals of humanism and of the Enlightenment, for it is found most of all among those who have remained faithful to the humanist tradition, while at the same time they feel the necessity of finding a new spiritual basis which may protect it against the standardized mass-civilization of the new age. Consequently they retain the old rationalist hostility to the idea of the supernatural and the transcendent. They have come to realize the dangers that a thoroughgoing scientific materialism or even a rationalism of the eighteenth-century type involves from the point of view of humanism. They are prepared to admit spiritual values and even the validity of mystical experience, but they still hold fast to the fundamental dogmas of naturalism—the denial of the transcendent and the conception of the universe as a closed order ruled by uniform scientific law. They seek a *natural* religion in the sense of a religion without metaphysic or dogma or relevation—a religion without God.

Now a religion of this kind would certainly possess the advantage of being easily reconcilable on the one hand with the ethical tradition of humanism and on the other with the world-view of scientific naturalism, but it does not follow that it would solve our religious problems or provide modern civilization with the spiritual dynamic of which it stands in need. For there are two factors to be considered. Just as it is possible to conceive of a religion which will satisfy man's religious needs without being applicable to the social situation of modern Europe—as, for example, in Buddhism—so we can construct, at least in theory, a religion which would be adapted to the social needs of modern civilization, but which would be incapable of satisfying the purely religious demands of the human spirit. Such a religion was constructed with admirable ingenuity and sociological knowledge by Comte in the nineteenth century, and it proved utterly lacking in religious vitality, and consequently also in human appeal. And a similar experiment which is being carried out with far less knowledge and greater passion by the modern Communists in Russia threatens to be even more sterile and inimical to man's spiritual personality.

It is useless to judge a religion from the point of view of the politician or the social reformer. We shall never create a living religion merely as a means to an end, a way out of our practical difficulties. For the religious view of life is the opposite to the utilitarian. It regards the world and human life *sub specie aeternitatis*. It is only by accepting the religious point of view, by regarding religion as an end in itself and not as a means to something else, that we can discuss religious problems profitably. It may be said that this point of view belongs to the past, and that we cannot return to it. But neither can we escape from it. The past is simply the record of the experience of humanity, and if that experience testifies to the existence of a permanent human need, that need must manifest itself in the future no less than in the past.

What, then, is man's essential religious need, judging by the experience of the past? There is an extraordinary degree of unanimity in the response, although, of course, it is not complete. One answer is God, the supernatural, the transcendent; the other answer is deliverance, salvation, eternal life. And both these two elements are represented in some form or other in any given religion. The religion of ancient Israel, for example, may seem to concentrate entirely on the first of these two elements—the reality of God—and to have nothing to say about the immortality of the soul and the idea of eternal life. Yet the teaching of the prophets is essentially a doctrine of salvation—a social and earthly salvation, it is true, but nevertheless a salvation which is essentially religious and related to the eternal life of God. Again, Buddhism seems to leave no room for God and to put the whole emphasis of its teaching on the second element—deliverance. Nevertheless, it is based, as much as any religion can be, on the idea of Transcendence. Indeed, it was an exaggerated sense of Transcendence that led to its negative attitude towards the ideas of God and the Soul. "We affirm something of God, in order not to affirm nothing," says the Catholic theologian. The Buddhist went a step further on the *via negativa* and preferred to say nothing.

Now, a concentration on these two specifically religious needs produces an attitude to life totally opposed to the practical utilitarian outlook of the ordinary man. The latter regards the world of man—the world of sensible experience and social activity—as the one reality, and is skeptical of anything that lies beyond, whether in the region of pure thought or of spiritual experience, not to speak of religious faith.

Christianity and the New Age

The religious man, on the contrary, turns his skepticism against the world of man. He is conscious of the existence of another and greater world of spiritual reality in which we live and move and have our being, though it is hidden from us by the veil of sensible things. He may even think, like Newman, that the knowledge of the senses has a merely symbolic value; that "the whole series of impressions made on us by the senses may be but a Divine economy suited to our need, and the token of realities distinct from them, and such as might be revealed to us, nay, more perfectly, by other senses as different from our existing ones as they are from one another."[1]

The one ultimate reality is the Being of God, and the world of man and nature itself are only real in so far as they have their ground and principle of being in that supreme reality. In the words of a French writer of the seventeenth century:

> It is the presence of God that, without cessation, draws the creation from the abyss of its own nothingness above which His omnipotence holds it suspended, lest of its own weight it should fall back therein; and serves as the mortar and bond of connection which

[1] *University Sermons*, p. 350. In this remarkable passage he develops a parallelism between the symbolic character of sensible knowledge and that of mathematical calculi and musical notation.

holds it together in order that all that it has of its Creator should not waste and flow away like water that is not kept in its channel.

Thus, although God is not myself nor a part of my being,

yet the relation of dependence that my life, my powers, and my operations bear to His Presence is more absolute, more essential, and more intimate than any relation I can have to the natural principles without which I could not exist . . . I draw my life from His Living Life . . . ; I am, I understand, I will, I act, I imagine, I smell, I taste, I touch, I see, I walk and I love in the Infinite Being of God, within the Divine Essence and substance. . . .

God in the heavens is more my heaven than the heavens themselves; in the sun He is more my light than the sun; in the air He is more my air than the air that I breathe sensibly. . . . He works in me all that I am, all that I see, all that I do or can do, as most intimate, most present, and most immanent in me, as the super-essential Author and Principle of my works, without whom we should melt away and disappear from ourselves and from our own activities.[2]

Or again, to quote Cardinal Bona, God is "the Ocean of all essence and existence, the very Being itself which contains all being. From Him all things depend; they

[2] *Chardon, la Croix de Jesus*, pp. 422, 423, in Bremond, *Histoire littéraire du sentiment religieux en France*, viii, pp. 21–2.

flow out from Him and flow back to Him and *are* in so far as they participate in His Being."[3]

Thus the whole universe is, as it were, the shadow of God, and has its being in the contemplation or reflection of the Being of God. The spiritual nature reflects the Divine consciously, while the animal nature is a passive and unconscious mirror. Nevertheless, even the life of the animal is a living manifestation of the Divine, and the flight of the hawk or the power of the bull is an unconscious prayer. Man alone stands between these two kingdoms in the strange twilight world of rational consciousness. He possesses a kind of knowledge which transcends the sensible without reaching the intuition of the Divine.

It is only the mystic who can escape from this twilight world; who, in Sterry's words, can "descry a glorious eternity in a winged moment of Time—a bright Infinite in the narrow point of an object, who knows what Spirit means—that spire-top whither all things ascend harmoniously, where they meet and sit connected in an unfathomed Depth of Life." But the mystic is not the normal man; he is one who has transcended, at least momentarily, the natural limits of human knowledge. The ordinary man is by his nature

[3] Bona, *Via Compendii ad Deum*.

immersed in the world of sense, and uses his reason in order to subjugate the material world to his own ends, to satisfy his appetites and to assert his will. He lives on the animal plane with a more than animal consciousness and purpose, and in so far, he is less religious than the animal. The life of pure spirit is religious, and the life of the animal is also religious, since it is wholly united with the life-force that is its highest capacity of being. Only man is capable of separating himself alike from God and from nature, of making himself his last end and living a purely self-regarding and irreligious existence.

And yet the man who deliberately regards self-assertion and sensual enjoyment as his sole ends, and finds complete satisfaction in them—the pure materialist—is not typical; he is almost as rare as the mystic. The normal man has an obscure sense of the existence of a spiritual reality and a consciousness of the evil and misery of an existence which is the slave of sensual impulse and self-interest and which must inevitably end in physical suffering and death. But how is he to escape from this wheel to which he is bound by the accumulated weight of his own acts and desires? How is he to bring his life into vital relation with that spiritual reality of which he is but dimly conscious and which

27

transcends all the categories of his thought and the conditions of human experience? This is the fundamental religious problem which has perplexed and baffled the mind of man from the beginning and is, in a sense, inherent in his nature.

I have intentionally stated the problem in its fullest and most classical form, as it has been formulated by the great minds of our own civilization, since the highest expression of an idea is usually also the most explicit and the most intelligible. But, as the writers whom I have quoted would themselves maintain, there is nothing specifically Christian about it. It is common to Christianity and to Platonism, and to the religious traditions of the ancient East. It is the universal attitude of the *anima naturaliter Christiana*, of that nature which the medieval mystics term "noble," because it is incapable of resting satisfied with a finite or sensible good. It is "natural religion" not, indeed, after the manner of the religion of naturalism that we have already mentioned, but in the true sense of the word.

It is, of course, obvious that such conceptions of spiritual reality presuppose a high level of intellectual development and that we cannot expect to find them in a pre-philosophic stage of civilization. Nevertheless, however far back we go in history, and however primitive is the type of culture, we do find evidence for the existence of specifically religious needs and ideas of the supernatural which are the primitive prototypes or analogs of the conceptions which we have just described.

Primitive man believes no less firmly than the religious man of the higher civilizations in the existence of a spiritual world upon which the visible world and the life of man are dependent. Indeed, this spiritual world is often more intensely realized and more constantly present to his mind than is the case with civilized man. He has not attained to the conception of an autonomous natural order, and consequently supernatural forces are liable to interpose themselves at every moment of his existence. At first sight the natural and the supernatural, the material and the spiritual, seem inextricably confused. Nevertheless, even in primitive nature-worship, the object of religious emotion and worship is never the natural phenomenon as such, but always the supernatural power which is obscurely felt to be present in and working through the natural object.

The essential difference between the religion of the primitive and that of civilized man is that for the latter the spiritual world has become a cosmos, rendered intelligible by philosophy and ethical by the tradition of the world religions, whereas to the primitive it is a spiritual chaos in which good and evil, high and low, rational and irrational elements are confusedly mingled. Writers on primitive religion have continually gone astray through their attempts to reduce the spiritual world of the primitive to a single principle, to find a single cause from which the whole development may be explained and rendered intelligible. Thus Tylor finds the key in the belief in ghosts, Durkheim in the theory of an impersonal *mana* which is the exteriorization of the collective mind, and Frazer in the technique of magic. But in reality there is no single aspect of primitive religion that can be isolated and regarded as the origin of all the rest. The spiritual world of the primitive is far less unified than that of civilized man. High gods, nature spirits, the ghosts of the dead, malevolent demons, and impersonal supernatural forces and substances may all co-exist in it without forming any kind of spiritual system or hierarchy. Every primitive culture will tend to lay the religious emphasis on some particular point. In Central Africa witchcraft and the cult of ghosts may overshadow everything else; among the hunters of North America the emphasis may be laid on the visionary experience of the individual, and the cult of animal guardians; and among the Hamitic peoples the sky-god takes the foremost place. But it is dangerous to conclude that the point on which attention is focused is the whole field of consciousness. The high gods are often conceived as too far from man to pay much attention to his doings, and it is lesser powers—the spirits of the field and the forest, or the ghosts of the dead—who come into closest relation with human life, and whose malevolence is most to be feared.

Consequently primitive religion is apt to appear wholly utilitarian and concerned with purely material ends. But here also the confusion of primitive thought is apt to mislead us. The ethical aspect of religion is not consciously recognized and cultivated as it is by civilized man, but it is none the less present in an obscure way. Primitive religion is essentially an attempt to bring man's life into relation with, and under the sanctions of, that other world of mysterious and sacred powers, whose action is always conceived as the ultimate and fundamental law of life. Moreover, the sense of sin and of the need for purification or catharsis is very real to primitive man. No doubt sin appears to him as a kind of physical contagion that seems to us of little moral value. Nevertheless, as we can see from the

history of Greek religion, the sense of ritual defilement
and that of moral guilt are very closely linked with one
another, and the idea of an essential connection between moral and physical evil — between sin and death,
for example — is found in the higher religions no less
than among the primitives. *Libera nos a malo* is a
universal prayer which answers to one of the oldest
needs of human nature.

But the existence of this specifically religious need in
primitive man — in other words, the naturalness of the
religious attitude — is widely denied at the present day.
It is maintained that primitive man is a materialist and
that the attempt to find in primitive religion an obscure sense of the reality of spirit, or, indeed, anything
remotely analogous to the religious experience of
civilized man, is sheer metaphysical theorizing. This
criticism is partly due to a tendency to identify any
recognition of the religious element in primitive
thought and culture with the particular theories of religious origins which have been put forward by Tylor
and Durkheim. In reality, however, the theories of the
latter have much more in common with those of the
modern writers whom I have mentioned than any of
them have with the point of view of writers who recognize the objective and autonomous character of

religion. All of them show that anti-metaphysical prejudice which has been so general during the last generation or two, and which rejects on *a priori* grounds any objective interpretation of religious experience. On the Continent there is already a reaction against the idea of a "science of religion" which, unlike the other sciences, destroys its own object and leaves us with a residuum of facts that belong to a totally different order. In fact, recent German writers such as Otto, Heiler, and Karl Beth tend rather to exaggerate the mystical and intuitive character of religious experience, whether in its primitive or advanced manifestations. But in this country the anti-metaphysical prejudice is still dominant. A theory is not regarded as "scientific" unless it explains religion in terms of something else — as an artificial construction from non-religious elements.

Thus Professor Perry writes: "The idea of deity has grown up with civilization itself, and in its beginnings it was constructed out of the most homely materials." He holds that religion was derived not from primitive speculation or symbolism nor from spiritual experience, but from a practical observation of the phenomena of life. Its origins are to be found in the association of certain substances, such as red earth, shells,

33

crystals, etc., with the ideas of life and fertility and their use as amulets or fetishes in order to prolong life or to increase the sexual powers. From these beginnings religion was developed as a purely empirical system of ensuring material prosperity by the archaic culture in Egypt and was thence gradually diffused throughout the world by Egyptian treasure-seekers and megalith-builders. The leaders of these expeditions became the first gods, while the Egyptian practices of mummification and tomb-building were the source of all those ideas concerning the nature of the soul and the existence of a spiritual world that are found among primitive peoples.

It is needless for us to discuss the archaeological aspects of this pan-Egyptian hypothesis of cultural origins. From our present point of view the main objection to the theory lies in the naive euhemerism of its attitude to religion. For even if we grant that the whole development of higher civilization has proceeded from a single center, that is a very different thing from admitting that a fundamental type of human experience could ever find its origin in a process of cultural diffusion. It is not as though Professor Perry maintained that primitive man lived a completely animal existence before the coming of the higher culture. On the contrary, the whole tendency of his thought has been to vindicate the essential *humanity* of the primitive. It is the claim of "the new anthropology" that it rehabilitates human nature itself and "disentangles the original nature of man from the systems, tradition, and machinery of civilization which have modified it."[4] If, then, primitive man is non-religious, the conclusion follows that human nature itself is non-religious, and religion, like war, is an artificial product of later development.

But this conclusion has been reached only by the forced construction that has been arbitrarily put upon the evidence. Because the primitive fetish has no more religious value for us than the mascot that we put on our motorcars, we assume that it can have meant nothing more to primitive man. This, however, is to fall into the same error for which Mr. Massingham rightly condemns the older anthropology — the neglect of the factor of degeneration. Our mascot is a kind of fetish, but it is a degenerate fetish, and it is degenerate precisely because it has lost its religious meaning. The religious man no longer uses mascots, though if he is a Catholic he may use the image of a saint. To the primitive man his fetish is more than the one and less

[4] H. J. Massingham, *The Heritage of Man*, p. 142.

than the other. It has the sanctity of a relic and the irrationality of a mascot. Professor Lowie has described how an Indian offered to show him "the greatest thing in the world"; how he reverently uncovered one cloth wrapper after another; and how at length there lay exposed a simple bunch of feathers—a mere nothing to the alien onlooker, but to the owner a badge of his covenant with the supernatural world. "It is easy," he says, "to speak of the veneration extended to such badges . . . as fetishism, but that label with its popular meaning is monstrously inadequate to express the psychology of the situation. For to the Indian the material object is nothing apart from its sacred associations."[5]

So, too, when Mr. Massingham speaks of primitive religion as "a purely supernatural machinery, controlled by man, for insuring the material welfare of the community," he is right in his description of facts, but wrong in his appreciation of values. To us, agriculture is merely a depressed industry which provides the raw material of our dinners, and so we assume that a religion that is largely concerned with agriculture must have been a sordid materialistic business. But this is entirely to misconceive primitive man's attitude to

[5] R. H. Lowie, *Primitive Religion*, p. 19.

nature. To him, agriculture was not a sordid occupation; it was one of the supreme mysteries of life, and he surrounded it with religious rites because he believed that the fertility of the soil and the mystery of generation could only be ensured through the cooperation of higher powers. Primitive agriculture was in fact a kind of liturgy.

For us nature has lost this religious atmosphere because the latter has been transferred elsewhere. Civilization did not create the religious attitude or the essential nature of the religious experience, but it gave them new modes of expression and a new intellectual interpretation. This was the achievement of the great religions or religious philosophies that arose in all the main centers of ancient civilization about the middle of the first millennium B.C.[6] They attained to the two fundamental concepts of metaphysical being and ethical order, which have been the foundation of religious thought and the framework of religious experience ever since. Some of these movements of thought, such as Brahmanism, Taoism, and the Eleatic philosophy, concentrated their attention on the idea of Being, while others, such as Buddhism, Confucianism, Zoroastrianism, and

[6] I have discussed this movement at greater length in *Progress and Religion*, ch. vi.

the philosophy of Heraclitus, emphasized the idea of moral order; but all of them agreed in identifying the cosmic principle, the power behind the world, with a spiritual principle, conceived either as the source of being or as the source of ethical order.[7] Primitive man had already found the Transcendent immanent in and working through nature as the supernatural. The new religions found it in thought as the supreme Reality and in ethics as the Eternal Law. And consequently, while the former still saw the spiritual world diffused and confused with the world of matter, the latter isolated it and set it over against the world of human experience, as Eternity against Time, as the Absolute against the Contingent, as Reality against Appearance, and as the Spiritual against the Sensible.

This was indeed the discovery of a new world for the religious consciousness. It was thereby liberated from the power of the nature daimons and the dark forces of magic and translated to a higher sphere—to the Brahma-world—"where there is not darkness, nor day nor night, not being nor not-being, but the Eternal alone, the source of the ancient wisdom," to the

---

[7] This may not appear obvious in the case of Buddhism. It is, however, implicit in the doctrine of Karma as the ground of the world process.

Kingdom of Ahura and the Six Immortal Holy Ones, to the world of the Eternal Forms, the true home of the soul. And this involved a corresponding change in the religious attitude. The religious life was no longer bound up with irrational myths and non-moral taboos; it was a process of spiritual discipline directed towards the purification of the mind and the will—a conversion of the soul from the life of the senses to spiritual reality. The religious experience of primitive man had become obscured by magic and diabolism, and the visions and trances of the Shaman belong rather to the phenomena of Spiritualism than of mysticism. The new type of religious experience, on the other hand, had reached a higher plane. It consisted in an intuition that was essentially spiritual and found its highest realization in the vision of the mystic.

Thus each of the new religio-philosophic traditions —Brahmanism, Buddhism, Taoism, and Platonism— ultimately transcends philosophy and culminates in mysticism. They are not satisfied with the demonstration of the Absolute; they demand the experience of the Absolute also, whether it be the vision of the Essential Good and the Essential Beauty, through which the soul is made deiform, or that intuition of the nothingness and illusion inherent in all contingent being

which renders a man *jivana mukti*, "delivered alive."
But how is such an experience conceivable? It seems to
be a contradiction in terms—to know the Unknow-
able, to grasp the Incomprehensible, to receive the Infinite. Certainly it transcends the categories of human
thought and the normal conditions of human experience. Yet it has remained for thousands of years as the
goal—whether attainable or unattainable—of the religious life; and no religion which ignores this aspiration can prove permanently satisfying to man's spiritual needs. The whole religious experience of mankind—indeed, the very existence of religion itself—
testifies, not only to a sense of the Transcendent, but
to an appetite for the Transcendent that can only be
satisfied by immediate contact—by a vision of the supreme Reality. It is the goal of the intellect as well as
of the will, for, as a Belgian philosopher has said, "The
human mind is a *faculty in quest of its intuition*, that is to
say, of assimilation with Being," and it is "perpetually
chased from the movable, manifold and deficient towards the Absolute, the One and the Infinite, that is,
towards *Being pure and simple*."[8]

A religion that remains on the rational level and

[8] J. Maréchal, *Studies in the Psychology of the Mystics*, trans.
Algar Thorold, 1927, pp. 101, 133.

denies the possibility of any real relation with a higher order of spiritual reality, fails in its most essential function, and ultimately, like Deism, ceases to be a religion at all. It may perhaps be objected that this view involves the identification of religion with mysticism, and that it would place a philosophy of intuition like that of the Vedanta higher than a religion of faith and supernatural revelation, like Christianity. In reality, however, the Christian insistence on the necessity of faith and revelation implies an even higher conception of transcendence than that of the oriental religions. Faith transcends the sphere of rational knowledge even more than metaphysical intuition, and brings the mind into close contact with super-intelligible reality. Yet faith also, at least when it is joined with spiritual intelligence, is itself a kind of obscure intuition — a foretaste of the unseen — [9] and it also has its culmination in the mystical experience by which these obscure spiritual realities are realized experimentally and intuitively.

Thus Christianity is in agreement with the great oriental religions and with Platonism in its goal of spiritual intuition, though it places the full realization of that goal at a further and higher stage of spiritual

[9] Cf. Rousselot, *Les Yeux de la Foi*.

development than the rest. For all of them religion is not an affair of the emotions, but of the intelligence. Religious knowledge is the highest kind of knowledge, the end and coronation of the whole process of man's intellectual development. Herein they all differ profoundly from the conceptions of religion and religious experience that have been developed by modern European thinkers. For the modern mind no longer admits the possibility or the objective value of spiritual knowledge. The whole tendency of Western thought since the Renaissance, and still more since the eighteenth century, has been to deny the existence of any real knowledge except that of rational demonstration founded upon sensible experience. Intuition, whether metaphysical or mystical, is regarded as an irrational emotional conviction, and religion is reduced to subjective feeling and moral activity. Such a religion, however, can have no intellectual authority, and in consequence it also loses its social authority and even its moral influence. Civilization becomes completely rationalized and secularized, as may be seen from the last two centuries of European history.

Nevertheless, man cannot live by reason alone. His spiritual life, and even his physical instincts, are starved in the narrow and arid territory of purely rational consciousness. He is driven to take refuge in the non-rational, whether it be the irrational blend of spirituality and emotionalism that is termed romanticism, or, as is increasingly the case today, in the frankly sub-rational sphere of pure sensationalism and sexual impulse.

Today we are faced with the bankruptcy of rationalism and with the necessity of finding some principle of the religious order which can rescue us from the resultant confusion. One alternative is that of the late D. H. Lawrence, who accepts the failure of reason, and who seeks to find a basis for the religious consciousness not in spiritual intuition, but in that lower intuition of the senses and the physical life, the reality of which cannot be denied even by the rationalist. He writes:

> Come down from your pre-eminence, O mind,
>   O lofty spirit!
> Your hour has struck,
> Your unique day is over,
> Absolutism is finished in the human consciousness too.
>
> A man is many things: he is not only a mind.
> But in his consciousness he is twofold at least:
> He is cerebral, intellectual, mental, spiritual,
> But also he is instinctive, intuitive, and in touch.

*　　　　*　　　　*　　　　*　　　　*

Christianity and the New Age

> The blood knows in darkness, and forever dark,
> In touch, by intuition, instinctively.
> The blood also knows religiously,
> And of this the mind is incapable.
> The mind is non-religious.
>
> To my dark heart gods *are*.
> In my dark heart love is and is not.
> But to my white mind
> Gods and love alike are but an idea,
> A kind of fiction.[10]

This is, so it seems to me, the inevitable conclusion of the religious mind that no longer conceives the possibility of spiritual intuition or supernatural revelation. It is driven back upon the lower type of religious experience, which primitive man possessed when he worshipped the daimonic powers that seemed to rule his life. And yet, even so, Lawrence's position is not wholly consistent, for even the lower type of religious experience is in a real sense spiritual. It is the result of a spiritual intuition, even though that intuition is, as St. Paul says, in bondage to "the weak and beggarly elements" of nature. The religion of the blood of which Lawrence writes, the religion of pure sense and animal instinct, can only be attained by the unreflecting animal soul. If we were conscious of it, we should not

[10] *Pansies*, pp. 65–66.

have it. It is a true spiritual instinct which prompted Lawrence to revolt against the tyranny of "the white mind" and to seek a deeper wisdom than that of the rational consciousness; but, owing to the denial and repression of true spiritual intuition, it has been deflected into a false cult of the primitive and the physical which can afford no true solution to his problem.

This is fully realized by another writer, who has considerable sympathy with his point of view and who also seeks escape from the present *impasse* in a religious experience. Mr. J. Middleton Murry not only admits the possibility of a spiritual intuition, but makes it the center of his whole theory of life.

He recognizes the insufficiency of the modern scientific point of view that identifies reality with the physical and biological world. The human mind can only achieve unity with itself and harmony with the universe on the higher "metabiological" plane, in an experience which transcends both sensible and rational knowledge. This experience finds its highest expression in the life of Jesus, and thereby Jesus was the creator of a new series of values and the starting-point of a new phase in the evolution of humanity.

Nevertheless, Mr. Murry holds that the reality that

is apprehended in this way is not metaphysical or transcendent; it is simply the organic unity of nature, the
unity of biological being. There is no eternal and transcendent being which we can think of as divine, but
only the natural organism which is the product of the
evolutionary process. For Mr. Murry is an adherent of
the dogma of "emergence," a worshipper of the God
that we create as we go along.[11] God is a useful fiction,
a creature of the human mind, not the ultimate ground
of reality. This relativism, however, ill accords with
the absolutism of his theory of knowledge. It is difficult to see how we can attain to a metabiological plane
of consciousness and activity if there is no corresponding metabiological stage of being. For metabiological
activity implies metaphysical being, no less than biological activity involves physical being. We must either accept the reality and autonomy of spiritual being
or abandon the possibility of spiritual knowledge. It is
true that the intuition of unity of which Mr. Murry
speaks does not necessarily involve the belief in the
transcendent personal God of Christian doctrine. It has
more affinity with the monism of the Vedanta, or still

[11] It is true that he does not term this concept God. Unlike
Professor Alexander, he reserves that title to the transcendent
God of the old religions.

more with that of Taoism. But it does necessitate, no less than Taoism, the idea of an eternal transcendental principle which is the source and not the product of the cosmic process.

It may be objected that Mr. Murry's philosophy has in fact arisen directly from his spiritual experience, and, consequently, that it cannot be inconsistent with it. But this is not exactly the case. Certainly Mr. Murry's theory of the existence of metabiological values and of a higher form of knowledge than the purely rational springs directly from his experience. But this is not so with regard to his denial of the transcendent and the supernatural. That was due not to his mysticism, but to his adherence to the dogmas of scientific naturalism, and he has interpreted his experience to accord with these preconceived ideas.

He himself points out that his first reaction to his experience was purely religious — a conviction of spiritual reality and spiritual regeneration — and that his mature philosophy is not so much a logical consequence of his mystical experience as the means by which he succeeded in "disintoxicating" himself from it. It is conditioned throughout by his fundamental hostility to any form of supernaturalism — by his conviction that the introduction of the category of the supernatural involves "mental and spiritual suicide."[12]

This prejudice has been firmly implanted in the modern mind by two centuries of dogmatic naturalism, but it is difficult to understand its rational justification in the present instance. From the point of view of scientific mechanism there is certainly no room for the supernatural, but on that assumption Mr. Murry's category of the metabiological must also be excluded. The anti-supernaturalist view rests fundamentally on the hypothesis of a universe in which quality and value have no meaning and where everything is reducible to matter and energy. If we once admit the possibility of a mode of spiritual consciousness or being which transcends the biological, there seems no reason to regard the human mind as its only field of manifestation.

It is no less reasonable to suppose that the metabiological plane is the point at which a higher order of

[12] This dogmatic acceptance of naturalism has entered so deeply into Mr. Murry's mind that the very idea of the supernatural is rejected with a kind of sacred horror as a blasphemous impiety. He writes: "To introduce, or to be prepared to introduce, the category of the supernatural into my thinking would be mental and spiritual suicide. A world which at a certain point . . . ceased to belong to the natural order is no world for me, a man of the twentieth century, to contemplate or live in; it would be a cheap and vulgar world from which it would be my duty as a man to escape immediately." — *God*, p. 112.

being has inserted itself into the life of humanity than to suppose that it is a completely new order which has "emerged" from below. Even in the sensible world we have an example of the way in which a higher order of being can intervene to modify the natural development of a lower order. From the animals' standpoint, man himself is a supernatural being whose action governs their life in a mysterious way and who even creates, as it were, new creatures like the setter and the race-horse, and admits them to a certain participation in his own life. And why, then, is it irrational to believe that, as Plato says, mankind is "the flock of the Gods," that human life is susceptible to the influence of a higher power which fosters in it those new capacities and modes of being which we call spiritual and meta-biological? Such a belief may seem to us incredible, but it is not really irrational. It would indeed be strange if reality did not transcend man's comprehension qualita-tively as well as quantitatively. The refusal to admit this possibility rests not so much on reason as on the humanist prejudice which insists that the human mind is the highest of all possible forms of existence and the only standard of reality. It is this prejudice which pre-vents Mr. Murry from developing the full implications of his religious experience. He has recognized one truth that is vital for religion—that the path of human development must lie in the spiritual, not the physical, world, and that his nature is not wholly earthbound—that it has a window that is open to the infinite. But, on the other hand, he rejects the other truth that is equally vital—the transcendence and absoluteness of spiritual reality. The religious attitude is only possible in the presence of the eternal and the transcendent. Any object that falls short of this fails to inspire the sense of awe and self-surrender, which is essential to true religion. Man cannot worship himself, nor can he adore a Time God that is the creation of his own mind. As soon as he recognizes its fictitious character such an idea loses all its religious power. And for the same reason every attempt to create a new religion on purely rational and human foundations is inevitably doomed to failure.

Chapter III
The Claim of Christianity

If we accept the necessity of an absolute and metaphysical foundation for religion and religious experience, we still have to face the other aspect of the problem — namely, how this spiritual experience is to be brought into living relation with human life and with the social order. The ecstasy of the solitary mind in the presence of absolute reality seems to offer no solution to the actual sufferings and perplexities of humanity. And yet the religious mind cannot dissociate itself from this need, for it can never rest content with a purely individual and self-regarding ideal of deliverance. The more religious a man is, the more is he sensitive to the common need of humanity. All the founders of the world religions — even those, like Buddha, who were the most uncompromising in their religious absolutism — were concerned not merely with their private religious experience, but with the common need of humanity. They aspired to be the saviors and pathfinders—ford-makers, as the Indians termed them —who should rescue their people from the darkness and suffering of human life.

Nowhere is this social preoccupation more insistent than in the religious tradition of the West, and it is to be found even in the most abstract and intellectualist type of religious thought. It is to be seen above all in Plato, the perfect example of the pure metaphysician, who, nevertheless, made his metaphysics the basis of a program of political and social reform. Indeed, according to his own description in the Seventh Epistle it was his political interests and his realization of the injustice and moral confusion of the existing state which were the starting point of his metaphysical quest. But though Plato realized as fully as any purely religious teacher the need for bringing social life into contact with spiritual reality and for relating man's rational activity to the higher intuitive knowledge, he failed to show how this could be accomplished by means of a purely intellectual discipline. He saw that it was necessary on the one hand to drag humanity out of the shadow world of appearances and false moral standards into the pure white light of spiritual reality, and, on the other hand, that the contemplative must be forced to leave his mountain of vision and "to descend again to these prisoners and to partake in their toils and honors."[1] But, as he says, the spiritual man is at a disadvantage in the world of politics and business. The eyes that have looked upon the sun can no longer distinguish the shadows of the cave. The man who cares only for eternal things, who seeks to fly hence and to become assimilated to God by holiness and justice and wisdom, is unable to strive for political power with the mean cunning of the ordinary "man of affairs."[2] In fact nothing could show the impossibility of curing the ills of humanity by pure intelligence more completely than Plato's own attempt to reform the state of Sicily by giving a young tyrant lessons in mathematics. The political problems of the Greek world were solved not by the philosopher-king, but by condottieri and Macedonian generals, and the gulf between the spiritual world and human life grew steadily wider until the coming of Christianity.

In the East, however, the religious conception of life was victorious and dominated the whole field of culture. In India, above all, the ideal of spiritual intuition was not confined to a few philosophers and

[1] *Republic*, 519.
[2] *Theatetus*, 176.

53

mystics, but became the goal of the whole religious development. It was, as Professor de la Vallée Poussin has said, "the great discovery that has remained for at least twenty-five centuries the capital and most cherished truth of the Indian people." The man who cannot understand this cannot understand the religion of India or the civilization with which it is so intimately connected. It is, however, only too easy for the Western mind to misconceive the whole tendency of Indian thought. It is apt to interpret the teaching of the Upanishads on the lines of Western idealist philosophy, and to see in the Indian doctrine of contemplation a philosophic pantheism that is intellectualist rather than religious. In reality it is in Western mystics such as Eckart or Angelus Silesius rather than in philosophers such as Hegel or even Spinoza that the true parallel to the thought of the Vedanta is to be found. It leads not to pantheism in our sense of the word, but to an extreme theory of transcendence which may be termed super-theism. Western pantheism is a kind of spiritual democracy in which all things are equally God; but the "non-dualism" of the Vedanta is a spiritual absolutism in which God is the only reality. At first sight there may seem to be little practical difference between the statement that everything that exists is divine and the statement that nothing but the divine exists. But from the religious point of view there is all the difference in the world. For "if this transitory world be the Real," says a medieval Vedantist, "then there is no liberation through the Atman, the holy scriptures are without authority and the Lord speaks untruth. . . . The Lord who knows the reality of things has declared, 'I am not contained in these things, nor do beings dwell in Me.' "[3]

God is the one Reality. Apart from Him, nothing exists. In comparison with Him, nothing is real. The universe only exists in so far as it is rooted and grounded in His Being. He is the Self of our selves and the Soul of our souls. So far the Vedanta does not differ essentially from the teaching of Christian theology. The one vital distinction consists in the fact that Indian religion ignores the idea of creation and that in consequence it is faced with the dilemma that either the whole universe is an illusion—Maya—a dream that vanishes when the soul awakens to the intuition of spiritual reality, or else that the world is the self-manifestation of the Divine Mind, a conditional embodiment of the absolute Being.

[3] *Vivekachudamani* (attributed to Sankara), trans. C. Johnston, p. 41.

Hence there is no room for a real intervention of the spiritual principle in human life. The Indian ethic is, above all, an ethic of flight — of deliverance from conditional existence and from the chain of rebirth. Human life is an object of compassion to the wise man, but it is also an object of scorn. "As the hog to the trough, goes the fool to the womb," says the Buddhist verse; and the Hindu attitude, if less harsh, is not essentially different.

> Men are held by the manifold snares of the desires in the world of sense, and they fall away without winning to their end like dykes of sand in water. Like sesame-grains for their oil, all things are ground out in the mill-wheel of creation by the oil-grinders, to wit, the taints arising from ignorance that fasten upon them. The husband gathers to himself evil works on account of his wife; but he alone is therefore afflicted with taints, which cling to man alike in the world beyond and in this. All men are attached to children, wives and kin; they sink down in the slimy sea of sorrow, like age-worn forest-elephants.[4]

It is true that orthodox Hinduism inculcates the fulfillment of social duties, and the need for outward activity, but this principle does not lead to the transformation of life by moral action, but simply to the

[4] *Mahabharata*, xii, ch. 174, trans. L. D. Barnett.

fatalistic acceptance of the established order of things. This is the theme of the greatest work of Indian literature, the Bhagavad-Gita, and it involves a moral attitude diametrically opposed to that of the Western mind. When Arjuna shrinks from the evils of war and declares that he would rather die than shed the blood of his kinsfolk, the god does not commend him. He uses the doctrine of the transcendence and impassibility of true being to justify the ruthlessness of the warrior.

> Know that that which pervades this universe is imperishable; there is none can make to perish that changeless being.
> . . . [T]his Body's Tenant for all time may not be wounded, O Thou of Bharata's stock, in the bodies of any beings. Therefore thou dost not well to sorrow for any born beings. Looking likewise in thine own Law, thou shouldst not be dismayed; for to a knight there is no thing more blest than a lawful strife.[5]

The sacred order that is the basis of Indian culture is no true spiritualization of human life; it is merely the natural order seen through a veil of metaphysical idealism. It can incorporate the most barbaric and non-ethical elements equally with the most profound

---

[5] *Bhagavad-Gita*, ii., pp. 17, 30–31, trans. L. D. Barnett.

metaphysical truths; since in the presence of the absolute and the unconditioned all distinctions and degrees of value lose their validity.

The experience of India is sufficient to show that it is impossible to construct a dynamic religion on metaphysical principles alone, since pure intuition affords no real basis for social action. On the other hand, if we abandon the metaphysical element and content ourselves with purely ethical and social ideals, we are still further from a solution, since there is no longer any basis for a spiritual order. The unity of the inner world dissolves in subjectivism and skepticism, and society is threatened with anarchy and dissolution. And since social life is impossible without order, it is necessary to resort to some external principle of compulsion, whether political or economic. In the ancient world this principle was found in the military despotism of the Roman Empire, and in the modern world we have the even more complete and far-reaching organization of the economic machine. Here indeed we have an order, but it is an order that is far more inhuman and indifferent to moral values than the static theocratic order of the Oriental religion-cultures.

But is there no alternative between Americanism and Orientalism, between a spiritual order that takes no account of human needs and a material order that has no regard for spiritual values? There still remains the traditional religion of our own civilization: Christianity, a religion that is neither wholly metaphysical nor merely ethical, but one that brings the spiritual world into vital and fruitful communion with the life of man.

The whole spiritual inheritance of European civilization is based upon Christianity, and even today whatever there is of religious life and spiritual aspiration in the West still draws its vitality from Christian sources.

Nevertheless it must be admitted that for centuries Christianity has been progressively losing its hold on Western culture, and both its doctrines and its moral ideals have fallen into discredit. The causes of this state of things lie deep in that process of the humanization and rationalizing of Western culture which I described in the earlier part of this essay. Ever since the Renaissance the centrifugal tendencies in our civilization have destroyed its spiritual unity and divided its spiritual forces. The Western mind has turned away from the contemplation of the absolute and the eternal to the knowledge of the particular and the contingent. It has made man the measure of all things and has sought to emancipate human life from its dependence on the supernatural. Instead of the whole intellectual and social order being subordinated to spiritual principles, every activity has declared its independence, and we see politics, economics, science and art organizing themselves as autonomous kingdoms which owe no allegiance to any higher power.

And these tendencies were not confined to the secular side of life; they made themselves felt in religion also. Religion came to be regarded as one among a number of competing interests — a limited department of life, which had no jurisdiction over the rest. And as it lost its universal authority, it lost its universal vision; it became sectionalized and rationalized with the rest of European life. The ancient unity of Christendom fell asunder into a mass of warring sects, which were so absorbed in their internecine feuds that they were hardly conscious of their loss of spiritual vision and social authority. In Catholic Europe, it is true, the Church maintained its universal claims and its absolute metaphysical principles, but there also it was gradually extruded from the control of social and intellectual life, and forced to concentrate itself on the inner defenses of the altar and the cloister. By the nineteenth century the forces of secularism and "anti-clericalism" were everywhere triumphant, and the new Latin democracies seemed bent on the creation of a purely "lay" culture, which should eliminate the last traces of religious influence from the national life.

But it is in Northern Europe that we can most clearly trace the disintegrating effects of modern culture within Christianity itself. Here Catholicism was replaced by a new conception of Christianity that gave free scope to the centrifugal tendencies of the Western mind. Protestantism eliminated the metaphysical element in the Christian tradition. It abolished asceticism and monasticism; it subordinated contemplation to action and the intelligence to the will. God was no longer conceived as the Super-essential Being, from Whom the created universe receives all that it has of reality and intelligibility, but as a "magnified non-natural man, who likes and dislikes, knows and decrees, just as a man, only on a scale immensely transcending anything of which we have experience."[6]

It is true that Luther's own religious experience was both genuine and profound, but it was not the positive intuition of the contemplative; it was a dark and tormented sense of man's utter helplessness and of the otherness of the Divine Power. For his discarding of

[6] Matthew Arnold, *St. Paul and Protestantism*, p. 14.

the intellectual element in religion had brought his mind back, as it were, to the religious attitude of primitive man who sees the Divine as an unknown and hostile power from which he recoils in terror. "Yea," he writes,

> God is more terrible and frightful than the Devil, for he dealeth with us and bringeth us to ruin with power, smiteth and hammereth us and payeth no heed to us. 'In His majesty He is a consuming fire.' For therefrom can no man refrain; if he thinketh on God aright his heart in his body is stricken with terror. . . . Yea, as soon as he heareth God named he is filled with trepidation and fear.
>
> For He assaileth a man and has such a delight therein that He is of His Jealousy and Wrath impelled to consume the wicked.[7]

But Luther's personal attitude is decidedly abnormal and nonrepresentative; the normal Protestant religious experience is of the milder and more emotional type represented by pietism and revivalism. Here faith is no longer conceived as a super-rational knowledge founded on the Divine Reason, but as a subjective conviction of one's own conversion and justification, and in place of the spiritual ecstasy of the mystic, who realizes his own nothingness, we have the self-conscious attitude

[7] Quoted by R. Otto in *The Idea of the Holy*, pp. 102–103.

of the pietist, who is intensely preoccupied with his own feelings and with the moral state of his neighbor. And this substitution of the ideal of pietism for those of asceticism and mysticism eventually led to the weakening and discrediting of the ethical ideals of Christianity, just as sectarianism undermined its social authority. However unjust may be the popular caricature of the pietist as a snuffling hypocrite of the type of Tribulation Wholesome or Zeal-of-the-Land Busy or Mr. Chadband, there can be no doubt that Puritan and Evangelical pietism succeeded in making religion supremely unattractive in a way that medieval asceticism had never done.

And, at the same time, the divorce of dogma at once from ecclesiastical tradition and from philosophy eventually left it helpless before rationalist criticism. It is true that nothing could have been further from the intention of the Reformers. In fact, it was the very vehemence of their conviction of the absolute transcendence and incomprehensibility of the Divine action that led them to reject alike the supernatural authority of the Church and the natural rights of human intelligence, and to fall back on the testimony of personal experience and the infallible authority of Scripture. But, though they succeeded in erecting on these foundations a system of dogma more rigid and more exclusive than that which it replaced, the whole dogmatic edifice rested on an arbitrary subjective basis and had no internal coherence or consistency. It incorporated a great part of the traditional patristic and scholastic theology, which really formed an organic element of the Catholic tradition that it professed to reject. Hence, as Harnack has shown, the work of the Reformation was confused and incomplete, and produced at first merely an impoverished version of traditional Catholicism. It required a long process of criticism and historical inquiry before the kernel of Protestant doctrine could be freed from its husk of traditional dogma.

With the advance of historical scholarship in the nineteenth century, it finally became clear that the dogmatic tradition of Christianity could not be separated from its ecclesiastical and sacramental elements. Catholicism was not, as the Reformers believed, the result of the apostasy of the medieval Papacy; it was a continuous process of organic development which is as old as Christianity itself. And so the modern Protestant scholar, who admitted that Christianity and Catholicism were identical down to the age of the Reformation, that "the Christianity of the apostolic age is itself incipient Catholicism, and that the Catholicizing of Christianity begins immediately after the death of Jesus," was forced to reject the Reformation compromise. He was left with the choice of two alternatives—either to deny the organic unity of the whole development and to view Christianity as mere syncretism—"a varying compound of some of the best and some of the worst elements of Paganism and Judaism, molded in practice by the innate character of certain peoples of the Western world,"[8] as Huxley puts it—or else to go back behind the early Church, behind even the New Testament, to the original purity of the gospel of Jesus.

This second alternative is the Liberal Protestant solution, and it is the logical conclusion of the appeal of the Reformers from the Church to the Bible and of their attempt to set up an abstract ideal of primitive Christianity against the historic reality of the Catholic Church. In the moral teaching of the Gospel and in the personality of "the historical Jesus" the Liberal Protestants believed that they had at last found a firm basis for a faith that should be purely ethical and religious without any contamination of metaphysics or

[8] T. H. Huxley, *Essays*, v., p. 142.

theological speculation. This is what Harnack means when he says that the work of the Reformation is only completed when *faith cancels dogma*, and that the Reformation is the end of dogma as the Gospel was the end of the Law. The divorce of dogma from intelligence that was inaugurated by the Reformers consummates itself in the dissolution of dogma itself in the interests of that moral pragmatism which is the essence of modern Protestantism. Christianity, it is said, is not a creed but a life; its sole criterion is the moral and social activity that it generates. And thus religion loses all contact with absolute truth and becomes merely an emotional justification for a certain standard of behavior.

But this intensely subjective attitude to religion is no less inconsistent with a genuinely historical understanding of the Gospels than it is with theology or metaphysics. Liberal Protestantism selects those elements in the Gospel which appeal to the modern liberal mind, and disregards or rejects the uncompromising supernaturalism on which the ethical teaching of Jesus rests. It condemned the Catholic tradition for replacing the historical Jesus by a metaphysical abstraction—the incarnation of a Divine hypostasis—while its own interpretation was nothing but an ethical abstraction—the incarnation of the ideals of liberal humanitarianism.[9]

It was inevitable that the one-sidedness of the Liberal Protestant solution should produce a corresponding reaction, and at the beginning of this century advanced criticism turned abruptly to the opposite extreme. The eschatological school was inspired by a justifiable distrust of the Liberal tendency to interpret the life of Jesus in terms of modern thought and sentiment, and they were consequently led to depreciate the ethical element in the Gospel and to accentuate its catastrophic and apocalyptic character. In Dean Inge's words, "They stripped the figure of Jesus

[9] The following passage from Mr. C. E. M. Joad's *The Present and Future of Religion* (p. 43) is a typical if somewhat extreme example of this attitude. "For many men of advanced ideas, today, Christ is primarily a great preacher and teacher of conduct, expounding doctrines of compelling force and originality. As such he despises ritual and ceremony, and lays stress upon what men do. He is a communist and an internationalist, advocating the widening of the private family to include the whole family of mankind. He is humanitarian, denouncing punishment, crying for mercy instead of vengeance, and insisting, if only as a utilitarian measure, on counteracting evil, not with a contrary evil, but with good. Above all, he is a socialist, insisting on the organic conception of society, and affirming that we are members of one another in so intimate a sense that the misery and degradation of one are the misery and degradation of all." But "we realize regretfully that Christ's dream of a regenerated world is too lovely for the little minds that run the machine of instituted religion."

of all the attributes with which the devotion of centuries had invested it and have left us with a mild specimen of the Mahdi type, an apocalyptic dreamer whose message consisted essentially of predictions about the approaching catastrophic 'end of the age,' predictions which of course came to nothing."

Thus we are left with two contradictory solutions, neither of which affords any basis for an explanation of the emergence of Christianity in the form in which it is known to history. Hence it is not surprising that those, like Loisy, who have followed the path of criticism to its extreme conclusion, should have ended in the despairing skepticism of a completely negative theory of religious syncretism. But even in this final stage there is no finality. All the resources of comparative religion are at the disposal of the critic, and the figure of the historical Jesus disappears in an ever-changing mist of Oriental myths and Hellenistic mystery religions. Neo-Pythagoreanism, Orphism, Iranian soteriology, the mystery religions, Mandaeanism: in each of them some scholar has found the key to the origins of Christianity, and each successive solution is equally convincing or unconvincing, for in this phantom world all things are shadows, and the shadows change their shape as the spectator changes his position.

The Claim of Christianity

We may well ask how it is that the relatively simple story of the birth of Christianity, concerning which, moreover, we possess fuller and more authentic documents than in the case of any other of the world religions, should have become involved in such a web of sophistication and misplaced ingenuity. And it would be incomprehensible were it not that the whole development has been conditioned from the outset by a series of *a priori* prejudices. The most obvious of them is the anti-metaphysical prejudice to which I referred in the last chapter — the refusal to admit the objective and autonomous character of religion and of spiritual reality, and the affirmation that everything in the world is *of the same color*, as Renan puts it, and that there is no free spiritual principle in the universe apart from the will of man. Hence it becomes necessary not only to eliminate every supernatural element in the Gospel and in the history of the Church, but, furthermore, to deny the essential originality and spontaneity of Christianity and to explain it away as a composite development derived from elements that were already in existence.

This prejudice has had an incalculable influence on the modern mind, since it could invoke the prestige of "science," that is to say, the dogmatic conception of scientific materialism. But its influence might have been limited to rationalist circles had it not been reinforced by a second prejudice, which was based on religious preconceptions. This was the Protestant conviction that a vital breach had intervened between the Gospel of Jesus and the Faith of the Church. The Reformers, it is true, placed this breach as late as the Middle Ages, but, as we have seen, the growth of historical knowledge gradually increased the antiquity of the Catholic development until its origins became actually coterminous with the foundation of Christianity as an organized religion. Thus the way is laid open for the acceptance of the rationalist explanation of Christian origins, excluding only the person of Jesus and an ethical abstraction of His teaching, which are preserved as an isolated and unrelated ideal of spiritual religion that is to inspire the religious life of modern men.

The moral earnestness and erudition of the advocates of this view have caused its fundamental illogicality and its unhistorical character to be overlooked, and even at the present day it enjoys enormous prestige, for it offers a *via media* between traditional Christianity and pure rationalism that appeals both to the Christian who has lost his faith in the dogmatic teaching of the Church and to the rationalist who has preserved a sense of religious values. It has recently found a distinguished adherent in Mr. Middleton Murry, who bases his own theory of religious naturalism on the personality and the religious ideal of Jesus. But Mr. Murry, at least, is more logical or more honest than his predecessors in that he does not claim the name of Christianity for his new religious ideal. On the contrary, he explicitly recognizes the inseparable connection between the Christian religion and the Christian Church. "There is not," he writes,

> and never will be any reconciliation between Christianity and the experimental method. Christianity is the great Church and nothing else is Christianity. To call anything else Christianity is to plunge into confusion and chaos; and it is an insult to Christianity. Christianity is a great thing, not a little one; one thing not many things; a rich thing not a poor thing; a majestic thing not a thing of shreds and patches. Christianity is Christianity at its noblest, truest, and most comprehensive, and that is the Catholic Church. If you desire to be a Christian, join it. It will make no demands upon you that are more fearful than the demands made upon you by any peddling form of Christianity. It asks no greater sacrifice than Little Bethel or the Church of England; and it does not insult your intelligence by inviting you to become a member of a contradiction in terms.[10]

[10] J. Middleton Murry, *God*, p. 229.

Christianity and the New Age

But when we have reached this point there is no longer any reason for one who is not under the influence of rationalist or Protestant prejudices to refuse to admit that the historic faith and life of the Church were founded on the life and gospel of the historic Jesus. It is, in fact, only so that we can account for the creative originality of the Christian religion. A great spiritual unity like Christianity cannot be the accidental product of a series of misunderstandings. It must have had its origin in some great spiritual force; and where is this to be found if not in the life of that Person whom even the rationalist admits to have been the greatest and most original religious genius in the history of humanity?

And as soon as we set aside these *a priori* conceptions and approach the study of Christian origins with an open mind, the vital relation between the Church and the teaching of Jesus at once becomes manifest. Christianity did not arise *in vacuo* as an abstract theory of salvation, like Buddhism or the Gnostic sects; it was organically and consciously linked with a pre-existing historic religion; and this religion alone among the great faiths of the world was essentially based on the belief in a Holy Society. The One God had chosen for Himself one people and had bound it to Him by an eternal covenant. Israel was a theophoric community; not only a witness to the Divine unity but the bearer of the Divine purpose of mankind; for this little people "despised by man, the servant of rulers," was to be the source of a universal Kingdom of God, which should embrace all nations, and in which the creative purpose of God should find its ultimate fulfillment. Thus Israel was not a nation in the ordinary sense so much as a church, and the loss of political independence under the Roman Empire tended still further to accentuate its religious aspect. Faced by the universalism of the Roman world-power, the spiritual universalism of Israel acquired yet clearer consciousness, and the mind of the people was preoccupied, as never before, by the hope of the coming of a Messianic deliverer who would break the power of the nations and set up the eternal kingdom of prophecy.

It was to those who lived in the expectation of this hope and "waited for the consolation of Israel" that the preaching of Jesus was addressed. His gospel consisted essentially in the announcement of the coming of the Kingdom; and this was not, as so many moderns hold, merely a figurative expression for an abstract ethical ideal; it was an absolutely realist conception of the coming of a new supernatural order—the culminating event in the history of Israel and of the world. So far the eschatological school is right; their error consists in their tendency to interpret this teaching in the spirit of the apocryphal apocalypses rather than in that of the prophets, and in their depreciation of its spiritual and universal character. For the Kingdom of the gospels is not a national triumph of Israel over his foes; it is the mystical and spiritual reign of God in humanity. It is already immanent in the present order, which it is destined to transform and supersede—it is a leaven and a seed and a hidden treasure. It is open not to the Jews as such—the children of Abraham—nor to the Scribes and Pharisees, who observe meticulously all the outward prescriptions of the Mosaic law, but to the poor and the meek, the seekers after justice and those who follow the Son of Man in his sufferings and humiliation.

Nevertheless, the spirituality of the Kingdom does not imply that it was purely internal and individual. It retained the objective social character that it possessed in the prophetic tradition. It was to find its realization in and through a community. But this community was no longer the national church-state of Jewish history; it was a new Messianic society—the "little flock" of which the gospels speak.[11] The mission of Jesus consisted essentially in the foundation of this society, not by doctrine alone, but by an act of creative power. Nothing can be further from the colorless Liberal picture of Jesus as a great moral idealist than the figure of the Son of Man in the Gospels, filled with the consciousness of his Messianic office and inaugurating a new supernatural dispensation by the New Covenant of his voluntary sacrifice. All the mythological parallels invoked by rationalist critics from the vegetation cults of primitive peoples and the mystery religions of the Hellenistic world sink into insignificance by the side of the profound spiritual reality of the words of Jesus, "I have a baptism wherewith I am to be baptized and how am I straitened until it be accomplished?", or of that great scene in the Upper Chamber, which only the most arbitrary preconceptions can remove from its place in the most ancient and authenticated documents of primitive Christianity.

Nor is it possible to deny that the actual beginnings of the historic Christian Church were rooted in this doctrine of a new order inaugurated by the Death and Resurrection of Jesus and incorporated in a spiritual society. The outpouring of the Spirit on the disciples

[11] Luke 12:32.

at Pentecost was regarded as the fulfillment of prophecy and of the promises of Jesus to His apostles. For the possession of the Holy Spirit was the essential characteristic of the new society. It was, even more than Israel, a *theophoric* community, since it was the external organ of the Holy Spirit and enjoyed supernatural powers and authority. And at the same time the early Christians preserved the historical associations and the social self-consciousness of the Jewish tradition; they felt themselves to be a true people, "a chosen race, a royal priesthood, a holy nation." Such a conception is almost incomprehensible to the modern mind, which has become accustomed to treat religion as a matter for the individual conscience, and it is not surprising that Protestant thinkers, such as Dean Inge, should repudiate the very idea of the existence of an objective supernatural society.[12] But there is not the shadow of a doubt that the early Christians believed in it with an intense conviction and devotion as the very center and ground of their faith. To Hermas, the

[12] In *Christian Ethics and Modern Problems*, p. 138, he quotes a passage from Landor, which perfectly expresses this modern idea of religion as essentially a private matter. "Religion," says Landor, "is too pure for corporations. It is best meditated on in our privacy and best acted on in our ordinary intercourse with mankind." But Landor is a Deist rather than a Christian.

Roman prophet, the Church is the first-born of creatures, and it is for her sake that the world itself was made.[13] As Christ is the New Adam the Church is the New Eve, the mother of the new humanity. And this mystical conception of the Church was in no way inconsistent with a strict insistence on its corporate authority and discipline. Although the eyes of the Christian were fixed on the future glory of the Kingdom of Christ rather than on the present order of things, this future kingdom was organically connected with the visible hierarchical Church, in the same way that the Messianic kingdom of prophecy was associated with the historic Israel. Indeed the Church was itself the future kingdom in embryo. In the vision of Hermas it is a tower, which is being built of living stones brought from every quarter of the earth and thus the process of its construction is, in Newman's phrase, *the measure of the duration of the world*.

This faith in a holy society and in a historical process of redemption distinguished Christianity from all its religious rivals in the ancient world, and gave it the militant and unyielding quality that enabled it to triumph in its struggle with secular civilization. But this is not sufficient to explain its religious appeal. If it

[13] Hermas, *Vision* iv, p. 1; cf. II. *Clement*, xiv., 1, 2.

had been nothing more than this, it would have been merely a Jewish heresy or an apocalyptic sect of the type that we actually find in Ebionism or Montanism. But in addition to the social and historical side of its teaching, Christianity also brought a new doctrine of God and a new relation of the human soul to Him. Judaism had been the least mystical and the least metaphysical of religions. It revealed God as the Creator, the Lawgiver and the Judge, and it was by obedience to His Law and by the ritual observances of sacrifice and ceremonial purity that man entered into relations with Him. But the transformation by Jesus of the national community into a new universal spiritual society brought with it a corresponding change in the doctrine of God. God was no longer the national deity of the Jewish people, localized, so to speak, at Sinai and Jerusalem. He was the Father of the human race, the Universal Ground of existence "in Whom we live and move and are." And when St. Paul appealed to the testimony of the Stoic poet, he recognized that Christianity was prepared to accept the metaphysical inheritance of Hellenic thought as well as the historic revelation of Jewish prophecy.

This is shown still more clearly in St. John's identification of the Logos and the Messiah in the prologue to the Fourth Gospel. Jesus of Nazareth was not only the Christ, the Son of the Living God; He was also the Divine Intelligence, the Principle of the order and intelligibility of the created world. Thus the opposition between the Greek ideal of spiritual intuition and the Living God of Jewish revelation — an opposition that Philo had vainly attempted to surmount by an artificial philosophical synthesis — finally disappeared before the new revelation of the Incarnate Word. As St. Augustine has said, the Fourth Gospel is essentially the Gospel of contemplation, for while the first three evangelists are concerned with the external mission of Jesus as Messianic King and Savior and teach the active virtues of Christian life, St. John is, above all, "the theologian" who declares the mysteries of the Divine Nature and teaches the way of contemplation.[14] Jesus is the bridge between Humanity and Divinity. In Him God is not only manifested to man, but vitally participated. He is the Divine Light, which illuminates men's minds, and the Divine Life, which transforms human nature and makes it the partaker of Its own supernatural activity.

Hence the insistence of the Fourth Gospel on the sacramental element in Christ's teaching,[15] since it is

[14] *de Consensu Evangelistarum* i., cap 3–5.
[15] *E.g.,* John 3:5; 6:32–58.

through the sacraments that the Incarnation of the Divine Word is no longer merely a historical fact, but is brought into vital and sensible contact with the life of the believer. So far from being an alien magical conception superimposed from without upon the religion of the Gospel, it forms the very heart of Christianity, since it is only through the sacramental principle that the Jewish ideal of an external ritual cult becomes transformed into a worship of spiritual communion. The modern idea that sacramentalism is inconsistent with the "spiritual" or mystical element in religion, is as lacking in foundation as the allied belief in an opposition between religion and theology. It is only when we reduce theology to religious rationalism and spiritual religion to a blend of ethics and emotion that there is no place left for sacramentalism; but under these conditions genuine mysticism and metaphysical truth equally disappear. Each of them forms an essential element in the historical development of Christianity. In the great age of creative theological thought, the development of dogma was organically linked with sacramentalism and mysticism. They were three aspects of a single reality—the great mystery of the restoration, illumination and deification of humanity by the Incarnation of the Divine Word. This is clearly recognized by Ritschl and his followers such as Harnack, although they involve mysticism, sacramentalism and scientific theology in a common condemnation.

Nevertheless, their criticism of the development of Greek Christianity is not entirely unjustified, for the historical and social elements, on which Ritschl laid so exclusive an emphasis, form an integral part of the Christian tradition, and apart from them the mystical or metaphysical side of religion becomes sterile or distorted. The tendency of the Byzantine mind to concentrate itself on this aspect of Christianity did actually lead to a decline in moral energy and in the spiritual freedom and initiative of the Church, and Eastern Christianity has tended to become an absolute static religion of the Oriental type.

It is true that this ideal, since it is a purely religious one, has much more in common with Catholic Christianity than have the secularized ideals of modern European culture. Catholicism and Orientalism stand together against the denial of metaphysical reality and of the primacy of the spiritual, which is the fundamental Western error. As Sir Charles Eliot has truly said,

> The opposition is not so much between Indian thought and the New Testament . . . the fundamental contrast is rather between both India and the New

Testament, on the one hand, and, on the other, the rooted conviction of European races, however much orthodox Christianity may disguise their expression of it, that this world is all-important. The conviction finds expression not only in the avowed pursuit of pleasure and ambition, but in such sayings as that the best religion is the one that does most good, and in such ideals as self-realization or the full development of one's motive and powers. Though monasteries and monks still exist, the great majority of Europeans instinctively disbelieve in asceticism, the contemplative life and contempt of the world.[16]

And yet, for all this, there is no getting over the profound differences that separate Christianity from the purely metaphysical and intuitive type of religion.

Against the Oriental religions of pure spirit, which denied the value and even the reality of the material universe, the Church has undeviatingly maintained its faith in a historical revelation that involved the consecration not only of humanity but even of the body itself. This was the great stumbling-block to the Oriental mind, which readily accepted the idea of an Avatar or of the theophany of a divine Eon, but could not face the consequences of the Catholic doctrine of the Two Natures and the full humanity of the Logos made flesh. This conception of the Incarnation as the bridge

[16] C. Eliot, *Hinduism and Buddhism*, Vol. I., p. ix.

between God and Man, the marriage of Heaven and Earth, the channel through which the material world is spiritualized and brought back to unity, distinguishes Christianity from all the other Oriental religions, and involves a completely new attitude to life. Deliverance is to be obtained not by a sheer disregard of physical existence and a concentration of the higher intellect on the contemplation of pure Being, but by a creative activity that affects every part of the composite nature of man. And this activity is embodied in a definite society, which shares in the divine life of the Spirit, while at the same time it belongs to the visible order of social and historical reality.

Thus Catholic Christianity occupies an intermediate position between the two spiritual ideals and the two conceptions of reality which have divided the civilized world and the experience of humanity. To the West its ideals appear mystical and other-worldly, while in comparison with the Oriental religions it stands for historical reality and moral activity. It is a stranger in both camps and its home is everywhere and nowhere, like man himself, whose nature maintains a perilous balance between the worlds of spiritual and sensible reality, to neither of which it altogether belongs. Yet by reason of this ambiguous position the Catholic

Christianity and the New Age

Church stands as the one mediator between East and West, between the ideal of spiritual intuition and that of moral and social activity. She alone possesses a tradition that is capable of satisfying the whole of human nature and that brings the transcendent reality of spiritual Being into relation with human experience and the realities of social life.

Chapter IV
Christianity and the New Order

It is clear from what has gone before that Christianity is not to be identified either with ethical idealism or with metaphysical intuition. It is a creative spiritual force, which has for its end nothing less than the re-creation of humanity. The Church is no sect or human organization, but a new creation—the seed of the new order which is ultimately destined to transform the world. Such, at least, is the Catholic belief, and though the non-Catholic may deny the reality of this faith and the supernatural character of this life, he cannot shut his eyes to the fact that they have actually had a profound influence on the course of history and have been one of the main sources of the spiritual achievement of European civilization. For, notwithstanding the materialism and secularism that have always been present in our culture, and which today seem everywhere triumphant, that achievement has been perhaps the most remarkable that the world has ever known. Europe is not a true racial or geographical unity; it is, in its essence, a spiritual community, and even its vast material expansion in modern times would have been impossible without the moral force and spiritual inspiration that it owes ultimately to the Christian faith.

However secularized a civilization may become, it can never entirely escape from the burden of its spiritual inheritance. Péguy has said of the Jews that they are a people which has no natural love of spiritual adventures. They ask only to be left alone, like other peoples, to dwell in their own land, to grow rich and to enjoy the good things of life. But the prophetic destiny with which their religion has charged them has forced them time after time against their will to leave their comfortable security and to go out into exile and the wilderness. And the same thing is true of Christendom: it cannot escape from the contagion of the divine fire that has been kindled in its midst.

Why is it that Europe alone among the civilizations of the world has been continually shaken and transformed by an energy of spiritual unrest that refuses to be content with the unchanging law of social tradition which rules the Oriental cultures? It is because its religious ideal has not been the worship of timeless and changeless perfection, but a spirit that strives to incorporate itself in humanity and to change the world. In the West the spiritual power has not been immobilized in a sacred social order like the Confucian State in China or the Indian caste system. It has acquired social freedom and autonomy, and consequently its activity has not been limited to the religious sphere but has had far-reaching effects on every aspect of social and intellectual life.

These secondary results are not necessarily of religious or moral value from the Christian point of view, for they may be deflected and distorted by the social medium through which they pass or contaminated by materialism and selfishness. But the fact remains that they are secondary and dependent on the existence of a spiritual force, without which they either would not have been or would have been utterly different.

For example, the Industrial Revolution, which appears at first sight one of the most materialistic aspects of Western civilization, would have been impossible without the moral earnestness and sense of duty that were generated by the Puritan ideal—an ideal far removed from that of Catholic Christianity, but one that owed its existence to a one-sided and sectarian interpretation of the Christian tradition.

And this is true also of the Renaissance and the humanist culture, in spite of the secularism and naturalism which seem so characteristic of them. The more one studies the origin of humanism the more one is brought to recognize the importance of an element which is not only spiritual, but definitely Christian. The old conception of the Renaissance as a revival of paganism—an idea which was popularized by nineteenth-century writers such as Burckhardt and J. A. Symonds—is today rejected not only by philosophers like Berdyaev, but by historians and critics, such as Karl Burdach and Giuseppe Toffanin. The Renaissance had its origin not only in the recovery of classical antiquity, but in the mystical humanism of St. Francis and Dante. The element survives in the later Renaissance in such representative figures as Francesco Pico and Marsilio Ficino, Botticelli and Michelangelo, Sadoleto and Tasso; and it finds a clear expression in the poems of Campanella, above all in his great canzone "Della possanza dell'uomo," in which the purely humanist ideal of man's power and glory is united with the Christian conception of the Divine Humanity.

It may be said that this is only one aspect and that not the most important of the humanist movement. But even the purely naturalistic achievements of the

Renaissance were dependent on its Christian antecedents. Humanism was, it is true, a return to nature, the rediscovery of man and the natural world. But the author of the discovery, the active principle in the change, was not the natural man; it was Christian man, the human type that had been produced by ten centuries of ascetic discipline and intensive cultivation of the inner life. The great men of the Renaissance were spiritual men, even when they were most deeply immersed in the temporal order. It was from the accumulated resources of their Christian past that they acquired the spiritual energy to conquer the material world and to create the new secular culture. It is true that the disparity between the source and the object of their activity tended to produce a sense of strain and spiritual tension, which is perceptible in the work of typical Renaissance geniuses such as Shakespeare and Cervantes, as well as in definitely religious characters like Michelangelo or Campanella. But, at least in Catholic Europe, the two elements had attained to a relatively stable equilibrium by the end of the sixteenth century, and had an equal share in the development of the later Renaissance culture. The spirit of Christian humanism dominated the whole of the seventeenth century and manifested itself alike in the Baroque art of Spain and

Christianity and the New Age

Italy and Central Europe, in the Jacobean and Caroline literature of England and in the classical culture of France. This religious current which runs through seventeenth-century culture cannot be set aside as a reactionary or negative phenomenon, for it lies at the heart of the higher civilization of the time and is responsible for some of its greatest achievements. Indeed, when in the eighteenth century this equilibrium was destroyed by the final victory of the naturalistic and rationalist tendencies, it involved the fall of the Renaissance culture itself. The new humanism of the Enlightenment was lacking in the vitality and spiritual depth of the earlier type. The one-sided rationalism of the Encyclopedists provoked the one-sided subjective emotionalism of Rousseau and the Romantics. And though both rationalism and romanticism were in a sense the heirs of the Renaissance tradition, neither of them was the true representative of the earlier humanism. Rationalism had lost its spiritual inspiration and romanticism lacked its intellectual order and its sense of form.

Thus the disappearance of the Christian element in humanism has involved the loss of its vital quality. If we attempt to resuscitate it on a purely naturalistic foundation, we may get something like the humanism of Anatole France, but we shall certainly not recover the creative humanism of the Renaissance period. This is admitted by the protagonist of the new humanism, Professor Babbitt, who fully realizes that every culture is a spiritual order and that humanism is only possible if we throw over naturalism and return to spiritual principles. But, while he recognizes that the very survival of Western civilization depends "on the appearance of leaders who have rediscovered in some form the truths of the inner life and repudiated the errors of naturalism," he is unwilling to make a complete return to the metaphysical and religious foundations. He prefers a kind of spiritual positivism based on the accumulated moral wisdom of the great historic traditions—Greek, Buddhist and Confucian. His desire to be "modern and individualistic and critical" causes him to shrink from committing himself absolutely to that which is eternal and universal.

Yet without such an affirmation, no true spiritual order is possible. Each of the great spiritual traditions to which he appeals rested on a metaphysical foundation, and if this is removed their moral order falls with it. Even Epicurus himself had to pass beyond the "flammantia moenia mundi" before he could bring peace to the minds of his disciples. By his insistence on the critical and individualistic attitude, Professor Babbitt is taking his stand on the weakest point in his position. The tradition of critical individualism still survives; indeed the modern intellectual has carried it to its extreme limits. But this excess is a last desperate reaction against the all-pervading pressure of a collectivist civilization. In the days of Voltaire the critic was leading a victorious advance against the routed forces of the old order; today he is fighting for his very existence against the ruling tendencies of the age. It is easier to restore a spiritual purpose to civilization than to reverse its tendency towards collectivism and solidarity. To a critic like Babbitt, Christianity is unacceptable on account of its weakness during the last two centuries against the dissolvent forces of rationalist criticism; but this type of criticism is already losing its power. The modern criticism of organized religion is in part the survival on a lower cultural plane of the rationalist thought of a past age, and in part a reaction against the romantic and individualist forms of religion that were characteristic of the nineteenth century or at least of the post-Reformation period. But Christianity in itself is in no way bound up with the individualist culture that is passing away. It was in origin a religion of order and solidarity which throve in an atmosphere of anonymity and collectivism. It was not itself responsible for the dying down of classical culture, the loss of civic liberty and the inauguration of the regime of compulsion and state socialism, which were, on the contrary, the necessary consequences of the inherent inconsistencies and weakness of the later classical culture itself. But it was able to accommodate itself to conditions in which a purely secular type of individual culture must inevitably perish.

And it seems possible that Christianity may survive modern humanism in the same way that it survived ancient Hellenism. However seriously Christianity is threatened by the materialism and mechanicism of modern civilization, it is in a much stronger position than the tradition of critical intellectualism, which can find neither a material nor a spiritual basis in the new conditions of life. The latter belongs essentially to the culture of a leisured class — not the new plutocracy of millionaires and leaders of industry, but the privileged classes of the old Europe, whether bourgeois or aristocratic, who stood outside the economic arena. This class has already practically disappeared, and its civilization and ideals of life are bound to disappear in like manner. The choice that is actually before us is not between an individualistic humanism and some form of collectivism, but between a collectivism that is purely mechanistic and one that is spiritual. Spiritual individualism is incapable of standing out against the collectivism and standardization of modern life: it is only by a return to spiritual solidarity that modern civilization can recover the spiritual principle of which it stands so greatly in need.

It will no doubt be objected, by the modernist and the medievalist alike, that there is a fundamental and insurmountable contradiction between the Christian ideal of spiritual freedom and the scientific determinism and materialism that are inherent in the new order. But we must make a distinction between the metaphysical determinism of the dogmatic materialist or "naturalist" and the physical determinism of the scientist, which is nothing but a recognition of the uniformity of physical laws within their proper limits. And what is this but the Hellenic belief in the existence of a universal cosmic order, which was accepted by the Christian Fathers as a necessary consequence of the creative activity of the Divine Word, which orders and disposes all things in number and weight and measure?

Consequently the material organization of the world by science and invention is in no sense to be refused or despised by the Catholic tradition, for to the Catholic philosopher no less than to the scientist the progressive *rationalization* of matter by the work of scientific intelligence is the natural vocation of the human mind. This must seem a hard saying when we consider that science and discovery, like a second eating of the forbidden fruit of knowledge, have proved a curse rather than a blessing to humanity. But the disease of modern civilization lies neither in science nor in machinery, but in the false philosophy with which they have been associated. At the very moment that man was at last acquiring control over his material environment, he was abandoning the ideal of spiritual order and leaving the new economic forces to develop uncontrolled without any higher social direction. Economic activity was no longer regarded as a function of society as a whole, but as an independent world in which the only laws were the purely economic ones of supply and demand, and of the relations between population and capital. Money and commodities were not considered in relation to social life, but became hypostatised into abstract principles on which social life was dependent.

But though these ideas accompanied the rise of the machine order, they are in reality profoundly inconsistent with that order and with the scientific genius, and today they are either dead or in the process of dissolution. It is now generally recognized—even by those who attach no importance to spiritual values—that the machine order involves social direction and that it is absurd to build up an elaborate artificial mechanism of production and to leave society itself at the mercy of private acquisitiveness. This was first clearly realized by the Socialists, and today Communism claims to be the only social theory that is consistent with the new scientific order. But Communism is itself a result of the same pseudo-scientific rationalism which produced the doctrine of Ricardo, and it gained consistency only by carrying the false principles of the older theory to their extreme conclusion. The old economists had excluded human values from economic life, but they had not attempted to deny them entirely. Outside business hours "the economic man" was free to behave as a human being. But to the Communist no such dualism is possible. The economic life absorbs the whole man and the whole society. The political, intellectual and spiritual aspects of life are all subordinated to the economic end, which alone is absolute and consequently is the only ethical criterion. Thus man becomes the servant and not the master of the machine, since society exists for economic production and man exists for society.

But the history of Communism is itself sufficient to disprove this materialistic conception of history. For

Christianity and the New Order

Communism was not the spontaneous product of impersonal economic forces. It had its origin in the mind of that atrabilious arch-individualist, Karl Marx, and the forces that inspired him were neither of the economic nor the material order. It was the instinct of spiritual self-assertion, the revolutionary ideal of abstract justice, and perhaps more than all the ineradicable Jewish faith in an apocalyptic deliverance that drove him from his own country and the interests of his bourgeois career to a life of exile and privation. Thus Communism, like every other living power in the world of men, owes its existence to spiritual forces. If it were possible to eliminate these, as the Communist *theory* demands, and to reduce human life to a purely economic activity, mankind would sink back into barbarism and animality. For the creative element in human culture is spiritual, and it triumphs only by mortifying and conquering the natural conservatism of man's animal instincts. This is true above all of science, for the path of the scientist leads him further from the animal than the rest of men. He lives not in the concrete reality of sensible experience, like the animal or the savage, but in a rarefied atmosphere of mathematical abstraction in which the ordinary man cannot breathe. If the materialist interpretation of history were true, the scientific intellectualization of nature could no more have arisen than could the metaphysical intuition of reality, and without science there could be no machine order. The true Marxian Communism is not that of a machine order which is the work of the creative scientific spirit, but rather that of the Eskimo, which is the direct product of economic necessity. For the machine is a proof not of the subordination of mind to matter, but of the subordination of matter to mind. So far from necessitating the substitution of material for spiritual order, it is itself a vindication of spiritual order, since it frees man from his age-long *animal* condition of dependence on nature and material circumstance.

But if the scientific order is to realize this ideal, it must be related to spiritual ends and must form part of a wider spiritual order. Material organization alone is incapable of saving civilization. Left to itself it may easily become a destructive force which is hostile alike to spiritual values and to human freedom. True civilization is essentially a spiritual order, and its criterion is not material wealth, but spiritual vision. It seeks a *Theoria*—an intuition of reality which is expressed in metaphysical thought and bears fruit in artistic creation and moral action. Thus Chinese civilization culminates in the metaphysical vision of cosmic law and in the ethical ideal of the Confucian just man; Indian civilization in the metaphysical vision of absolute being and in the moral ideal of the Sadhu; and Hellenic civilization in the vision of the intelligible world and in the ethical ideal of the philosopher.

In Christianity the idea of spiritual order acquires a yet wider and more profound significance. It is based upon the belief in a divine society which transcends all states and cultures and is the final goal of humanity. For as a modern Thomist has written, "The human personality is not entirely contained in political society; it belongs above all by its innermost and truest being, by its spiritual element, to another and more perfect society, to the universality of being, the World-Whole which includes the living Infinite, God Himself, as its Universal Good and Sovereign Head; and political society, however wide and numerous it may be, is but a minute section of this immense and innumerable Republic,"[1] this city of God of which St. Augustine and St. Thomas speak. This society exists in the nature of things as "the republic of all men under the law of God,"[2] although the actual disorder of human nature

[1] T. Bésiade, *La Justice générale,* in *Mélanges thomistes*, 1923, p. 334.
[2] St. Thomas, Sum. Th. i–ii, q. 100, a. 5.

prevented its effective realization by man. It has therefore been reconstituted on a higher plane by the Incarnation, through which mankind is united in a direct and personal relation with the Divine Word. And this new unity is something more than a society; it is an organism, a living body whose head is Christ the Word and whose vital principle is the Divine Spirit.

> But this great society is not yet made; it is in the making—in process of becoming—it grows under the guidance of Christ, Whose mystical Body has not yet attained its full stature, to its immanent perfection, that is to say, to the perfect possession of God; it is a universal gravitation towards God 'Who turns all things to the love of Himself.' . . .
>
> And it depends on us to push the universe with all our powers towards its sublime destiny, to contribute in our degree and for our part to the promotion and perfection of the kingdom of God.[3]

If this is the idea that should inspire Christian culture, it may well be asked whether a Christian civilization has ever existed. It is surely not to be found in the theocratic absolutism of the Byzantine East, nor in the feudal barbarism of the medieval West, nor in the humanism of the Renaissance. Yet through all their manifold imperfections each of them has aspired to it in

[3] Bésiade, *op. cit.*, p. 340.

their fashion, and if our own civilization is to recover a spiritual principle, it is here that we must seek it. The essential achievement of our culture—the conquest of material order—is not, as we have seen, inconsistent with this ideal. In fact it may be regarded as its natural complement, for the restoration of man to his true position as the master of nature and the organizer of the material world, which is the function of science, corresponds in the natural order to the spiritual restoration of human nature in itself, which is the work of Christianity in the supernatural order.

In a Christian civilization the scientific order would no longer offer, as it does at present, the tragic spectacle of vast resources of power and intelligence devoted to producing unsightly and unnecessary objects and to endowing mankind with new means of self-destruction; it would become an instrument for the realization of man's true destiny as the orderer of material things to spiritual ends. And so, too, with regard to the international aspects of our civilization. Without spiritual order the cosmopolitanism of modern culture does not make for peace; it merely increases the opportunities of strife. It destroys all that is best and most distinctive in the local and national cultures, while leaving the instincts of national and racial hostility to develop unchecked. It unites mankind in the common enjoyment of the cinema and the Ford car and the machine gun without creating any spiritual unity. The recovery of the Christian idea of order would give a spiritual expression to the universality of modern culture. Its material unification would become subservient to the ideal of the spiritual unity of mankind in justice and charity, an ideal that has a very real attraction for the modern mind, but which secular idealism is powerless to achieve.

We must make our choice between the material organization of the world — based either on economic exploitation or on an economic absolutism, which absorbs the whole of life and leaves no room for human values — and the Christian ideal of a spiritual order based on spiritual faith and animated by charity, which is the spiritual will. The triumph of such an ideal in a world that seems governed only by material forces and distracted by hatred and greed may seem a fantastic dream, but is it any more hopeless than the enterprise of that handful of unknown and uneducated men from a remote Oriental province who set out to conquer the imperial power of Rome and the intellectual culture of Hellenism? In history it is often the incredible that happens — *credo quia impossibile* has been justified again and again. Sooner or later it is inevitable that men's minds should turn once more in search of spiritual reality, and when once the tide begins to flow all the sandcastles that we have built during the ebb disappear.

Every Christian mind is a seed of change so long as it is a living mind, not enervated by custom or ossified by prejudice. A Christian has only to *be* in order to change the world, for in that act of being there is contained all the mystery of supernatural life. It is the function of the Church to sow this divine seed, to produce not merely good men, but spiritual men — that is to say, supermen. In so far as the Church fulfills this function it transmits to the world a continuous stream of spiritual energy. If the salt itself loses its savor, then indeed the world sinks back into disorder and death, for a despiritualized Christianity is powerless to change anything; it is the most abject of failures, since it serves neither the natural nor the spiritual order. But the life of the Church never fails, since is possesses an infinite capacity for regeneration. It is the external organ through which the Spirit enters the social process and builds up a new humanity — *populus qui nascetur quem fecit Dominus*. The spirit breathes and they are created and the face of the earth is renewed.

BIOGRAPHICAL NOTE
Christopher Dawson (1889-1970)

Externally, the life of Christopher Dawson was uneventful; internally, in the life of the mind, great events took place. For Dawson could integrate large masses of historical data into an understandable unity and make this the basis for his sharply etched interpretations of the movement of history. He could make the events of history stand out clearly in the light of a broad historical vision—a vision which also sees what is below the surface of history and discovers the deeper meaning of historical developments.

Christopher Dawson was assisted in this task by his power of poetic penetration, shown in striking metaphors that deepen the reader's comprehension and appreciation of what is being described. And he possessed a unique aptitude for choosing quotations that support his interpretation of a movement, an event, or a personality, and provide a decisive conclusion to the argument he is making.

These natural talents were complemented by the circumstances of his birth, which heightened his awareness of seemingly disparate cultural elements and motivated him to discover their unity. For—on October 12, 1889—Christopher Dawson was born of an English father and a Welsh mother in Hay Castle, near the border between England and Wales. The coexistence in his own family of these two distinct national cultures developed Dawson's sense of cultural differences and of their significance, a theme which later came to play a very prominent role in his thought.

When Christopher Dawson was about six years old, his father, a retired army colonel, moved the family to his ancient ancestral residence in Yorkshire. This old manor house and its natural surroundings became Christopher's second childhood home and the source of associations which greatly influenced his later development.

Dawson attended Winchester public school and Trinity College, Oxford, where he majored in history, receiving his degree in 1911. His interest in Catholicism was stimulated by a visit to Rome in 1908, where he was fascinated by the Baroque art and architecture he found there. In addition, his father had a great interest in Dante and strong Anglo-Catholic sympathies. Christopher Dawson became a convert to the Catholic Church in early 1914.

Dawson did not publish his first book, *The Age of the Gods*, until 1928, when he was almost 40. As if to compensate for this late start, he published eight more books in the next seven years, including *The Making of Europe*, the book by which he is best known to students.

From 1940 to 1944 Dawson served as editor of *The Dublin Review*, a leading English Catholic periodical. At the University of Edinburgh in 1947–48 he became the first English Catholic to deliver the Gifford Lectures. Finally, from 1958 to 1962, he lectured at Harvard University as the first occupant of the Charles Chauncey Stillman Chair.

Christopher Dawson's published works eventually came to twenty-three, including two volumes of Gifford Lectures and two volumes based on lectures he had delivered at Harvard in the Stillman Chair. He died at Budleigh Salterton, a seacoast town in southwest England, on May 25, 1970.

It is probable that Christopher Dawson's greatest

value for readers today lies in his wide-ranging presentation of movements in world history, guided by the principles of the Christian conception of history. He thus supplies Christians with an effective response to modern non-Christian philosophers of history and to their influence on contemporary ideologies — men such as Hegel, Marx, and Nietzsche, and in our own century, Spengler and Toynbee and the numerous heirs of the Enlightenment.

At a time when Christianity is being strongly assaulted, both from without and from within, by the impact of alien ideologies, Dawson's work reasserts the Christian meaning of history, providing an interpretation that is both broader and deeper than anything which the ideologies have to offer.

SOPHIA INSTITUTE

Sophia Institute is a non-profit institution that seeks:

— to restore philosophy to its true identity as a systematic inquiry into eternal truths about the nature of things;

— to clarify man's understanding of himself as a free creature capable of knowing objective truth through natural reason;

— to elucidate the phenomenon of objective values and their relation to human happiness; and,

— to demonstrate the central role that philosophy can play in resolving many of the crucial questions that confront man today.

Sophia Institute Press

Sophia Institute Press serves these ends in a number of ways. It publishes translations of foreign works to make them accessible for the first time to English-speaking readers. It brings back into print many books that have long been out-of-print. And it publishes important new books that fulfill the ideals of Sophia Institute.

Sophia Institute Press publishes books on philosophy as well as interdisciplinary works on topics in the humanities. These works revive and deepen many of the insights of traditional philosophy and integrate them with the legitimate advances of subsequent philosophies. The books published by Sophia Institute Press afford readers a rich source of the enduring wisdom of mankind.

Sophia Institute Press makes high-quality books available to the general public at modest prices by using advanced cost-effective technology and by soliciting donations to subsidize general publishing costs. In these ways, Sophia Institute Press ensures that its books receive much wider distribution than more expensive editions published by profit-making publishers.

A free descriptive catalogue of books already published will be sent to you on request.

Your Part

Your generosity can help Sophia Institute Press provide the public with inexpensive editions of works containing the enduring wisdom of the ages. Please send your tax-deductible contribution to Sophia Institute Press, Box 5284, Manchester, NH 03108. Your questions, comments, and suggestions are also welcome.

Sophia Institute Press is a tax-exempt institution as defined by the Internal Revenue Code, Sections 501 (c) (3).

INDEX

Index

Index